Notes on Strategy and Logistics

You are holding a reproduction of an original work that is in the public domain in the United States of America, and possibly other countries. You may freely copy and distribute this work as no entity (individual or corporate) has a copyright on the body of the work. This book may contain prior copyright references, and library stamps (as most of these works were scanned from library copies). These have been scanned and retained as part of the historical artifact.

This book may have occasional imperfections such as missing or blurred pages, poor pictures, errant marks, etc. that were either part of the original artifact, or were introduced by the scanning process. We believe this work is culturally important, and despite the imperfections, have elected to bring it back into print as part of our continuing commitment to the preservation of printed works worldwide. We appreciate your understanding of the imperfections in the preservation process, and hope you enjoy this valuable book.

NOTES ON

STRATEGY AND LOGISTICS.

Brevet Major WILLIAM A. KOBBE,

Captain Third Artillery, U. S. Army,

INSTRUCTOR.

ARTILLERY SCHOOL PRESS
FORT MONROE, VIRGINIA.
1896

The following pages have been compiled from time to time for use with authorized text-books, books of reference, maps, &c , at the Artillery School, to establish, if possible, a common point of view from which to examine the opinions which these publications advance. To gain distinctness, the field of view is contracted, perhaps unduly, and many stock in trade principles of strategy are, perhaps indiscriminately, ignored. In preparing the notes for the printer, an effort was made to so connect subjects that one would lead naturally to the next.

FORT MONROE, VA., March, 1896.

I

INTRODUCTION. *The profession of arms.*—In the intercourse of the human race there are conflicts of interest which, if these be paramount, end in war. War is, therefore, a condition: it cannot be concisely defined and the many definitions proposed are elusive and vexing. He who follows the profession of arms need not concern himself with them.

For him it is enough to known that disputes between the most cultivated nations are settled ultimately by war and that success in the field establishes the standing of a people. He is familiar with the depressing story of nations sinking to decay when, in the pursuit of luxury and gain, they had lost the agressiveness which, wisely trained, defends that which is good and repels that which is evil; an agressiveness from which the noblest virtues have arisen.

Armies.—War, indeed, has been often savage and soldiers have been brutal: but in human affairs, whether in church or state, nothing has escaped the ferment of development. The same influences have modified and tempered warfare which are always at work to purify and elevate. The love of power and the fascination of conquest, once mainsprings of conflict, are now disreputable, and no power may employ its armed forces with these motives however well disguised. An army has become as much a conservator of peace as it is and has always been an instrument of war. Even the reproach that is an aggregation of non-workers which contributes nothing to the common wealth must fall since humane and enlightened methods have made of the army a school, of the officer a teacher and guardian, and of the soldier a pupil of the state. "To take a lad, before either stature, or gait, or habit is formed (often boorishly formed) and to give him an education at once physical and moral, to teach him to march, to ride, to fire, daily to pass many precious hours in the free open air, to give him habits of order, of precision, of cleanliness, of truth; to teach him how to obey and thus how to command; to tell him that he has duties which he owes to his country. and to redeem him at a critical age from idle frivolity" is to create a sterling citizen, an invaluable ingredient for the community to which he returns and on which he never will be a burden. A modern army produces producers.

An army, or at least a large army, it has been said, is dangerous to free institutions. Whether this was ever true or not it is not true now. In monarchial countries personal fealty and allegiance to the sovereign sometimes breeds a military caste which is unpopular and which may be hateful; but it is growing less and less easy to use it to refashion any established order endeared to a majority of the people In a republic,—in the United States,—this personal allegiance is diverted to flag and country and is lavished on these with impassioned loyalty and devotion No military caste is then possible unless, indeed, it be based on the respect for the army which it earns by hatred of intrigue and freedom from debasing influences.

The nature of war.—War is the employment of physical forces to render an adversary powerless to oppose a political object by overthrowing him. It is, therefore, a continuation of state policy after diplomacy and mediation have failed.

In this employment of physical force all recourses of the adversary must be attacked, not in anger but with method "The greatest kindness in war is to bring it to a speedy conclusion", hence "every idea of philanthropy in war is a most pernicious error." "The essence of war is violence and moderation in war is an imbecility."

The object of war may be attained short of actual physical overthrow of an adversary, for he may be brought to realize that he can, at best, postpone this result; or that success is improbable; or he may be gradually exhausted by the magnitude of his effort until public opinion reacts on state policy From these considerations spring the conceptions of the offensive and defensive

Extreme conceptions of it.—The nature of war may be examined by considering the esteem in which mastery in war is held. It is manifest at once that success in the field overrides every other form of prestige. This is, perhaps, partly due to a sentiment of gratitude, often extravagant ; for a nation at war is a nation in peril. but the unswerving verdict of the world for ages must be based on something more real than this. The extremes of popular and sometimes of professional opinion concerning the eminence of military talent disclose some confusion of ideas. It is held on the one hand that there is something occult and subtle in warfare into the mysteries of which a soldier to be successful must first be initiated and on the other that "we cannot conceive where those difficulties lie of which so much is said, and what that genius and those extraordinary mental powers required in a

General have really to do. All appears so simple, all the requisite branches of knowledge appear so plain, all the combinations so unimportant, that in comparison with them, the easiest problem in higher mathematics impresses us with a certain scientific dignity."

One due to the literature of war.—The first view is not held by anyone who has had any considerable experience in war it may be held and is held by many who have studied war, sometimes with intense interest and application, from books. There have been few great leaders and the inference seemed fair that these, who have often held the leading-strings of history, worked by superhuman methods which clever scrutiny and sifting might lay bare. This has been the origin of many books and much writing, stimulated during long periods of peace by the fascination of building up theories to fit the events of the most recent wars "and in this way it has been sought to establish maxims, rules and even systems for the conduct of war." This literature has been infinitely extended, directly, by official reports, narratives, memoires and histories, indirectly by those who cater to the popular interest in military affairs and who write for the sake of writing or for profit, what may be classified as pure romance and fiction.

The necessity for a guide in study.—The military reader or student who enters this field will be dismayed at its extent unless it be made clear to him that most of it is a barren waste which he may shun and that much which remains must be read with nice perception and judgement. An instructor, to be well equipped must be able to impart this faculty,* and he may insist at once on the general rule that those books should be unreservedly rejected which are not free from vague statement and military cant.

The literature of war. Official reports.—Except their official reports, memoires and narratives, leaders in war have been small contributors to this literature. The greatest leaders have, perhaps, contributed least of all. It would seem that official reports of subordinates should be the richest and freshest sources of reliable data, but they are not The best evidence of this is that they do not agree and that prominent incidents of the most important campaigns have remained matters of dispute. Every one knows that it is difficult to obtain from several eye witnesses accounts which are not at variance of common, every day events,—and that these are subjected to skillful and

---

* "I have studied history a great deal and often for want of a guide have been forced to lose considerable time in useless reading".—Napoleon

laborious sifting by experts to reach the truth Whatever may be the influences which cause this it is plain that they are infinitely more potent in war, while the flush of victory and chagrin of defeat tend to produce a state of mind which is neither judicial nor candid. Moreover official reports are made, so to speak, over the same last, with a conventional phraseology in which everything that has happened is fathered tacitly upon a common design. "Follow the working of the General's mind in the rear, whatever his rank. From the first moment the conduct of the fight has been taken out of his hands. Either too great preliminary extension or the hot-headedness of a subordinate, or a miscalculation, has precipitated matters, and beyond feeding up troops as fast as they arrive he has been powerless.* But the victory is won and he must write a report. Whatever he may have thought during the crisis, it is perfectly certain that with success will come a reaction of thankfulness to the troops engaged: and even if he was aware of what was actually going on in the fighting line all the time, he will forbear to refer to it, but will only refer to his gallant troops for having saved the day. But from these reports the official history is afterwards constructed " "According to the official history, at Gravelotte on the 18th of August, 43 companies of different regiments were at one and the same time in the Auberge of St. Hubert The building is scarcely large enough to contain a single company on war strength 43 companies are more than 10,000 men. Where were 9,800 men who had no room?"

Descriptive writing and fiction —Official reports are the genesis of military opinion and it is easy to trail them through history, historical romance and finally through pure fiction Whether the last be taken seriously or not it has been most potent in upholding false notions of what really takes place in war: and in fiction much should be included which is reported for the press. The smallest rivulet, much less a river, never "runs red with blood" and probably would not if soldiers fought in the water. Away from field hospitals, blood is conspicuous nowhere on the battlefield Many wounds bleed very little, the blood from others is quickly absorbed by the clothing and, if very profuse, by the earth. "Whole ranks" are never "mown down by shot" because, for one sufficient reason, anything like drill ground formations are absent in battle. A multitude of photographs taken immediately after battles show, with very

---

* "Dur... is of more harm than use I must then rely on my division ... I think and act with all my might to bring up my troops to the right place at the right moment, after that I have done my duty "—General Lee

few exceptions, that the dead lie widely distributed or here and there in small groups. The cries and groans of the wounded are sometimes distressing after an action but during its progress they are rarely heard. Many men are wounded, even severely, who do not discover it at once; others halt, quietly discard their accoutrements and sit down or seek shelter to examine the wound; only very few, outside of battle pictures, throw up their arms and fall forward. Even these are little noted in the rush and separation of battle and it is a common experience for men to afterwards seek for and find a dead comrade who has not been missed until the assembly and roll call

Inaccurate data in reports—St. Privat.—"In military science, just as in other sciences, accurate data are essential to the formation of sound opinions, yet perhaps nowhere is this necessity more frequently disregarded." The German official history of the war of 1870, has long been accepted as a plain and unassuming statement of events as they occurred, and so in one sense it is. But the inexperienced or unguided reader, whether historian or student, will receive impressions from it which are wide of the truth. It is due to this, for instance, that the attack of the Prussian Guard at St. Privat is famous and will be immortal and their loss is commonly stated as about 6000 out of 18,000 men in 10 minutes. The impression gained from the official account is that of a deliberately planned and well ordered attack in which the advance was made in regular tactical formations until on account of great losses the troops were directed to halt and hold the ground. This account has been "read" by an expert as follows, though without mention of the inextricable confusion and intermixing of the attacking troops or of the fact that owing to the extent of front no one portion could possibly be aware of the losses which were being suffered elsewhere. "About 5 o'clock in the afternoon the IXth corps (next on the right to the Guards) was being hardly pressed, and to relieve this pressure, Prince August of Wurtemberg ordered, after seeking the concurrence of the Commander-in-Chief, the two divisional commanders to attack the enemy." * * * . "The first troops to commence the attack were the 4th Guard Brigade, consisting of, in all, 26 companies, or about 5500 men deployed in two lines with skirmishers in advance Even during its deployment at St. Ail it was overwhelmed by a shower of bullets and almost immediately afterwards it broke into skirmishers and advanced by rushes. The attack came to a standstill about 600 paces from the enemy, but the men held their ground and did not retire They lay out in the open until the final advance, which took place some two hours later, repulsing with the aid of the artillery fire. the counter attack of the enemy's masses. When the final attack took place they accompanied it and continued fighting until far into the night Meanwhile the 1st Guard Brigade (about 5000 strong) had advanced from its position. southwest of St. Marie aux Chenes, still preserving its rendezvous formation, viz , three lines of company columns, about 120 yards apart, and proceeded to change direction to the left under a perfect rain of chassepot bullets. It then crossed the high road and continued to gain ground to the left, but the fire proved more than it could bear, the rear of the column pressed on to the front, and its change of front to the right does not appear to have been made as on parade. The attack so disastrously begun was pushed on with great courage, till within some 600 yards of the enemy, where its momentum died out, and like the 4th Brigade on its right, it lay down and held its own till the subsequent rush carried it on some two hours later. From the commencement of the movement, till the advance died out, about half an hour had elapsed Now referring to the talk of losses, we find that the 1st Guard Brigade lost altogether, during the whole day's fighting, 72 officers and 2100 men, the 4th Brigade almost exactly the same number or a fraction over 30 per cent of their respective strengths, in an action which lasted at least three hours and a half. Even if we assume half of the whole loss to have been suffered in the first half hour, the 6000 out of 18,000 in 10 minutes is reduced to 2000 out of 10,000 in half an hour; a very different state of things."

Obscure data— The charge at Nashville.—About 4 o'clock in the afternoon on the second day of the Battle of Nashville the Federal line made the charge which finally overthrew the enemy. It is instructive to trace the accounts of this charge in the official reports, from that of the Commanding General down through those of a portion of the line (General A. J. Smith's) which took the most conspicuous part in it. Most of the reports are dated a few days after the battle

General Thomas, Commanding the Army. "About 3 P M. Post's Brigade * * * was ordered by General Wood" (4th Corps) "to assault Overton's Hill. * * * Immediately following the effort of the Fourth Corps, General Smith's and Schofield's commands moved against the enemy's works, in their respective fronts carrying all before them" etc.

General A. J. Smith, Commanding Corps. "About 3 p. m

General McArthur" (commanding 1st Division) "sent word that he could carry the line on his right by assault Major General Thomas being present, the matter was referred to him and I was requested to delay the movement until he could hear from General Schofield, to whom he had sent. General McArthur not receiving any reply" (*i. e.* from General Smith) "and fearing that if the attack should be longer delayed the enemy would use the night to strengthen his works, directed the First Brigade to storm the hill."

General McArthur, Commanding 1st Division "Fearing that if delayed until next day the night would be employed by the enemy to our disadvantage, I determined to attack "

First Brigade, 1st Division

"At length General McArthur, tired with the long delay and fearful that the day would pass without making any serious impression upon the enemy's lines, directed me to withdraw my brigade and "take that hill."

Second Brigade 1st Division

"About 4 p m I received the order to assault the works in my front"

Third Brigade, 1st Division

"Between 3 and 4 p. m. I observed the right of the division—the First Brigade—advancing to charge the enemy's left, and quickly Colonel Hubbard's brigade, immediately on my right, started on the charge. Seeing that Colonel Hubbard ought to be supported, I ordered the brigade to follow and charge the works in our front "

12th Iowa Infantry

"About 3 p. m I was ordered to throw up an earthwork in my front, and procured tools and had my work half completed when at about 4 o'clock, a charge was commenced by the right of our division. I at once ordered my men to cease work and prepare for a charge, and a moment afterwards, being told that we were ordered to advanced, I gave the command forward."

35th Iowa Infantry.

"About 4 o clock p. m. the line moved forward."

7th Minnesota Infantry.

"Towards the close of the day a charge was made upon the enemy's works," * * * "My regiment moved forward with the line."

33rd Missouri Volunteers.

"We remaind in this position until about 3.30 p m., when we received orders to intrench for the night. While this order was being executed there was a general movement of the lines to our right, and a charge was made upon the rebel works."

General Garrard, Commanding 2nd Division. "Noticing about 4 p m., a heavy musketry fire on the right of the corps, and believing that the critical point in the battle had arrived, I gave the order for the whole division to charge. This order was most promptly obeyed."

First Brigade, 2nd Division.

"About 4 p. m., a charge was ordered."

Second Brigade, 2nd Division

"A few minutes before 4 p. m., everything being in readiness, General Garrard's order was received to charge the enemy's works."

58th Illinois Infantry.

"A fierce cannonading took place all along the line, during which the men lay close, till 3.15 p. m., when the First Division of our Corps having carried by assault the fortified hill which covered the enemy's left flank, the order to charge was passed along the line."

32nd Iowa Infantry.

"At 3 30 p. m. the right of the First Division carried the left of the enemy's works; we then moved forward at a double-quick over an open field, * * * and in a few minutes gained the intrenchments."

Third Brigade, 2nd Division

* * * "At about 3.30 p m. that portion of the command" (on the right) "commenced its final advance upon the enemy's works. It required but a moment to put my brigade in motion, and the whole command, with a shout peculiar to this corps, advanced."

(The Third Division took no part as a whole)

The Nashville Report Explained —Nashville was an all important if not a decisive battle. Thomas defeated, Sherman's march to the sea was neutralized and Hood free to operate in any one of several effectual ways. The fighting on the first day had been indecisive, so that the result of both days battle turned on this charge of the late afternoon of the second. No battle of the civil war has given cause for fewer differences of opinion or for less controversy as to facts than this; yet the historian framing his account of its climax and who turns with confidence to the official reports is perplexed with what he finds. The commander-in-chief writes as if he might be telling of something which he had not seen and which had been told to him. One of his corps commanders, Smith, makes it plain that neither he nor any of his colleagues ordered or authorized the charge Of Smith's two division commanders one, McArthur, in the absence of orders to the contrary directed one of his three Brigades to advance, while at almost the same moment the other Division Commander, Garrard, without instructions of any kind ordered his whole division to charge From the reports of brigade and regimental commanders it is clear that many of them took their cue from the movement of troops on either flank, two regiments suspending on this account important work which they had been ordered to carry out.

Here, then, is a good instance of the difficulty of forming correct military opinion from official reports. In case of defeat explanations may well differ· but this was a battle fought with great deliberation and which virtually wiped out the enemy's army. Sherman had reached the sea, the situation was rose colored for the North and commanders of all grades had undistracted leisure in which to review calmly the parts which they had taken and to make candid report.

Parts of the Nashville reports quoted are in fair accord; the student will simply be puzzled to interpret them taken all together. Most of all will he be disconcerted if he seek for deep-laid plan or common design. Other portions of the reports which need not be quoted show discrepancies which are curious and for which it is not easy to account. Thus the capture of a Confederate general officer is claimed in several of them,—two regimental commanders giving details and each adding the name and company of the private soldier of his regiment who made the capture One of them adds "I make this explanation as I am informed nearly every regiment in the command claims to have captured him." Finally, correspondent and story writer who, as has been said, are both potent in shaping popular judgement will find accounts of the capture of guns and flags, of individual gallantry and medals of honor which, with the help of some lawful imagination, will serve them well.

The voluminous reports and correspondence of the War of Secession compared with those of earlier and even later wars are, on the whole, very free from misleading statements and conventional false coloring: and this is true of both sides. There are, of course, many statements which clash and many more which should be read and construed with some discretion and allowances. The charge at Nashville, already cited, is a case in point. General Thomas had led his inadequate force back from Georgia with infinite skill, forethought and patience. At Nashville he took up a defensive position, received reinforcements, perfected his equipment and placed his troops in order of battle seemingly untroubled by popular clamor and by the pressing demands of his superiors for an immediate offensive advance. During both days battle he rode quietly from point to point, watchful and absorbed, giving few orders, making few changes, content to let well enough alone He had thought and acted with all his might to bring up his troops to the right place at the right moment, he knew his troops and he knew his corps commanders, he resisted frequent appeals from subordinates for reinforcements or for permission to take this or that initiative. At 3 o'clock on the second day Smith's line was 500 or 600 yards from the enemy, Thomas and Smith not a hundred yards in rear of it,—giving no orders, watching intently the skirmishers almost under the enemy's works. Both knew from three years schooling in war that in a little while from somewhere along the line would come the impulse which would launch it forward.

It is quite plain from the reports how this impulse came in due time from one of the two divisions commanders who led the way, orders or no orders. But General Garrard, the other division commander, reports that he ordered a charge at the same moment, inferentially, on his own account and unaware of McArthur's movement,—an order which at least one of his brigade commanders does not mention. Here then is a coincidence so uncommon that, unexplained, the situation is improbable. As a matter of fact, however, Garrard's report is strictly true, at least from his own standpoint, He knew instinctively, as even the soldiers in the ranks knew, that the critical moment had come and he ordered the charge. Two brigade commanders near him received the order in person and started toward their commands. The order for the 3rd and *nearest* brigade was carried at a gallop by an Aide who reached the line only to find it already breaking from cover and beginning the charge.

Accou... of ... wars not trustworthy These examples have been d... ... recent wars not because recent wars offer any which ... ... they do not; but because it is possible to examine them critically and to disprove this or that statement. To do this with earlier wars is at first difficult and soon becomes impossible. Indeed military history up to the beginning of this century had not passed very far beyond romance, and ere long an era is reached where it is little else than a budget of tales and stories brought from the battle field and spread abroad by word of mouth That latter-day reports of the doings of highly trained and highly organized armies should be at all misleading is, however, strange enough and adds by implication to the distrust with which older records must be met.

Late military literature—The latest reports if read and construed with some discretion and allowance are, in the main, frank and authentic and the latest military literature published largely in professional journals has, in consequence, done much to eradicate vicious dogmas and creeds in spite of stubborn traditions. Even the war correspondent of to-day is often a writer whose exact and spirited narrative and the charm of whose style bring him a multitude of readers.

The other extreme of opinion due to misconception.—The other extreme view of the eminence of military talent depreciates it, as has been pointed out, and is not confined to the unthinking or the unlearned· indeed the note of depreciation has been sounded very clearly by a brilliant writer whose books are read everywhere. "An unlearned person," he says, "might be inclined to suspect that the military art is no very profound mystery, that its principles are the principles of plain good sense; and that a quick eye, a cool head, and a stout heart will do more to make a general than all the diagrams of Jomini."

Why war is difficult.—Sever the irony and depreciation from this passage and it is quite true; for "in war everything is very simple but it is the simple things which are difficult " Macaulay's "quick eye, cool head, stout heart and plain good sense," is just a combination which is exceedingly rare. Their possession means the ability to exercise common sense amid constantly recurring emergencies, complications and chances, an ability which is the rarest of all "In war difficulties accumulate and produce a friction which no man can imagine who has not seen war. Through the influence of a thousand petty circumstances, which cannot properly be described, things disappoint us and we fall short of the mark. *It is because the circumstances cannot be described that there is so great a difference between real war and war on paper.* The military machine, the army and all belonging to it is, in fact, simple and appears on this account easy to manage. But it is composed entirely of individuals; no part of it is in one piece. and each individual part keeps up its own friction. This enormous friction, which is not concentrated as in mechanics at a few points, is everywhere brought in contact with chance and thus facts take place upon which it was impossible to calculate. *The knowledge of this friction is a chief part of that, so often talked of, experience in war which is required in a good general·* he must be aware of it that he may overcome it and that he may not expect a degree of precision in results which is impossible. Besides, it can never be learnt theoretically, and if it could, there would still be wanting that experience of judgment which is called tact. Through this experience and practice the idea comes to the mind of itself that such and such expedient will or will not suit.''

Chance and contingencies.—The chances and contingencies which have been mentioned are constantly crossing the commonplace situations of every day life, and anyone may note how some of the simplest designs are defeated daily by this or that accident which he could not forsee. Now in war analogous situations, differing only immeasurably in degree, are of daily and hourly occurrence· they represent the normal condition of affairs. and added to them all is the great element which is usually absent in daily life, the element of danger,—the element which requires the strong will and that moral and physical courage which can never be wanting in a consummate general.

Qualifications for war.—To meet these situations in the presence of danger requires self reliance, discrimination and good judgment, and the last must be so prompt that it may be considered an instinct or an impulse if not an inspiration Sometimes in minor affairs, men judge correctly without being sure that they have done so more rarely they judge correctly and are sure of it, although the evidence has been no better in one case than in the other. ''What is required of a leader is a certain unfailing power of discrimination which only knowledge of men and things can give. because a great part of the information obtained in war is contradictory, a still greater part is false and by far the greatest part is doubtful Only thus is explained how so often men have made their appearance in war whose pursuits had been previously of an entirely different nature· how indeed, distinguished generals have often not arisen from the very learned or erudite class of officers and how even great experience in war has often failed to produce a leader'' where the leaders temperament or where this or that qualification was wanting.

Special training not always recognized as necessary.—Something of confusion and a sense of depreciation concerning the qualities necessary in a general has been also bred by the fact that special qualities and special training were only gradually recognized as necessary. "It is not so long since that no state had made any provision for a complete separation of even the military and naval services The old leaders fought battles by sea as well as by land. Nor did the impulse which nautical science received at the end of the 15th century produce any material improvement in the division of labor. At Flodden the right wing of the victorious army was led by the Admiral of England. At Jarnac and Moncontour the Huguenot ranks were marshaled by the Admiral of France. Raleigh, highly celebrated as a naval commander, served during many years as a soldier in France, the Netherlands and Ireland. Blake distinguished himself by his skillful and valiant defense of an inland town before he humbled the pride of Holland and Spain on the ocean,—and great fleets were intrusted to Rupert who was renowned chiefly as a hot and daring cavalry officer."

Study and reflection—To enumerate the physical and mental qualities which a general should have would be misleading, because success depends mainly on a fortunate combination of some of them in proper proportions but great ability never exists without capacity for work, moral and physical courage and vigorous health. With these there must be a certain amount of study and experience. "If an officer has been accustomed to deal with military problems, even on paper, the powers of his mind will have been strengthened in the right direction and the process of reasoning which the solution of difficulties involves will come easier to him than to the man who has to depend on a rusty intelligence and the chance of a happy inspiration." "Study will not make a dull man brilliant nor confer resolution and rapid decision. but the quick, the resolute, the daring, will be able the more likely to decide and act correctly in proportion as they have studied the art they are called upon to practice." "A certain amount of study is absolutely necessary for any man who ever wishes to command troops in the field; the great thing is to read a little and think a great deal,—and think it over and over again."*

The persistent study of military history, especially that of modern times, will lead reflection and meditation in the right

---

*"It is not genius which reveals to me suddenly and secretly what I have circumstances unexpected by other people it is reflection it is meditation —Napoleon

channels if the student keep in mind that he is in search of lessons and not of models; and that in the conduct of war he will require wisdom, not learning, character, not intellect. "The theory of the art of war is valuable just in so far as it assists to guide a man through the vast labyrinth of military experience and to prepare his mind to be ready to act for itself under the emergencies of actual war, but it must renounce all pretension to accompany him on the field of battle."

Summary —It cannot be repeated too often that in war everything is simple but that these simple things are difficult It is hard to understand why this is not generally perceived and why it has led to any confusion of ideas, because it is the same in daily life and intercourse between man and man. There also the simplest things are difficult because they are innumerable and their relations form endless combinations which cannot be discerned The difference is only in this, that lack of discernment results in one case in inconvenience or unhappiness to individuals while in war it means disaster and perhaps ruin to the community. "It is owing to the tremendous consequences which follow in the train of war that men have invested their leaders with a whole equipment of science and arts,—or failing to find these have ascribed all success to genius and talent alone and denied all use of knowledge." As always, the truth lies between the extremes. "A certain stock of ideas, not inborn but acquired, is indispensible. at the same time this knowledge is of a different nature and is differently absorbed from that in all other arts and occupations. In these it is the result of daily and hourly continuous experience, in daily use; and results follow each other as one brick or stone is laid by its fellow in a building If the engineer calculates the strength of a pier the result is no emanation from his own mind and he operates by rules which he is not first obliged to discover.* But in war the commander must carry with him the whole mental apparatus and his knowledge must be completely assimilated with his mind and life," though he may not be aware from which book or from the study of which campaign he has acquired it.

War is a succession of emergencies and presents an uninterrupted series of new problems, and each class must be managed for itself. Moreover wars are few and far between and no one is like the other, and the commander must have his machine perfect w   in all its parts, on demand.

---

*It is 1   n   to plan a bridge than, e. g , to arrange a festivity the success of one can be assured, that of the other cannot

FUNDAMENTAL ELEMENTS OF ACTION.—Though precepts and formulas are of no avail in war and lead only to disaster, there are a few great elements of action which underlie every success. These are 1st. Definiteness of purpose. 2nd. Simplicity of plan. 3rd. Unity of action and 4th. Energy of execution

1. A purpose which is not well defined leads to hesitation, vacillation, councils of war and defeat · it is evident, also, that advantage will not be taken of those situations and circumstances which good fortune throws in the way of him who has a definite end in view. *Absolute inactivity is better than aimless action.*

2. Whatever plan is adopted should be as simple as possible and, while not too general, elastic enough to stand the strain of complications and contingencies which cannot be forseen. Plans whose success depends on combinations and cooperation are plausible and attractive. but they are the "pontes asinorum" of incompetency: cooperation does not cooperate and combinations do not work out if any one term fails.

3. Unity of action,—community of purpose, is already attained to some extent if the troops which compose armies are homogeneous,—*i. e.* of the same nationality and class actuated by the same motives and sympathies This great advantage the Confederates had over the Federals and every Confederate commander knew to what extent he could call on troops which reported to him from time to time from widely separated regions without first testing and observing them in action. A general should also communicate if not disclose the general features of his plans, with some discretion, at first to subordinate commanders and finally to as many as possible, even to the rank and file. That this, as a rule, is not done infers a lack of cleverly conceived projects and intentions or their absence altogether. In the War of Secession the object of a campaign, the troops to be met, the objective of a march or movement, were unknown from day to day and a thousand camp rumors, often exaggerated and alarming were constantly afloat. "The plan, at the moment of execution should be known to as many as possible of those who have to carry it out Far too often these things are wrapped in mysterious silence. At the moment of action if possible even the soldiers should know the plan, each then, even the private, helps intelligently." "It is needless to say that a temporary amount of reticence is requisite on the part of a general, but it is a mistake to carry this too far. Men will always work better w⁀ ⁀ ⁀ the exertion demanded of them is made app⁀ ⁀ ."

4. A plan, once adopted, must be executed ⁀ ⁀ ⁀ ing

energy and persistency. This is obvious and, it may appear, comparatively simple, but it is not. In war there is endless friction and a multitude of obstacles complicate and embarras matters and in the aggregate tend to tire men out Ordinary hardships repeated day after day, fatigue, lack of sleep, hunger and thirst, uncleanliness, lower the vital forces and affect the energies to an extent which no one can conceive without the experience. The strength and buoyancy of mind required to rise superior to these constitute fortitude,* and without fortitude all other soldierly qualities count for little.

DEFINITIONS DEDUCED FROM "OBSTACLES."—Nearly all writers on war have endeavored to define strategy and one definition may well be as true as any other. But while definitions are little else than "the mind playing with words," they are necessary in discussion, however feeble and inadequate they may be Fair, working definitions may be obtained, deductively, as follows

The art of war is the art of overthrowing an enemy by an armed force.

The means and methods of doing this are called the "operations of war" and the territory in which they are employed is called the "theatre of operations'

The operations of war consist in overcoming the natural and artificial obstacles which may be met

Natural obstacles are the climate and topographical features of the country. artificial obstacles are temporary and permanent fortifications, the troops of the enemy and, negatively, the necessity for supplying troops and providing for their security and repose.

Tactics may therefore be defined as the art of overcoming obstacles in the theatre of operations

Strategy may be defined as the art of selecting and occupying that theatre of operations which will admit of the most favorable employment of tactics.

Strategy in modern war intimately connected with logistics —This conception of strategy is especially applicable to modern war· it is, perhaps, not applicable at all to conditions of warfare which no longer exist. "The character of military operations is mainly determined by the nature of the armies engaged in them," by their military instruction, the weapons, and most of all by the necessity of supplying them and the means employed to do so To say, therefore, that "the great principles of strategy have remained unchanged" is a vague generality which means very

*"Not dangers, but discomforts prove a man"

little; and to enunciate them is to set forth a few of the most commonplace maxims The first question which now, as always, attracts the attention of a commander about to lead his army to war is the choice of a line of operations on which it will act, but to-day the considerations which determine his choice are resticted by the necessity he is under of providing at all times for the supply of food, forage and ammunition while at the same time directing it against the point which he is to strike.

"The possibilities and limitations in raising, feeding, supplying, arming, transporting and caring for armies, all of which are branches of logistics are, therefore, intimately related to strategy, 1st by the time which is required to organize the army for action including its recruiting training and the preparation of its various supplies 2nd, by the time which is required to move it to its sphere of action and to furnish it with all necessary supplies during its campaign 3rd, in so disposing the depots, means of transportation, communications, &c , that the movements of the army may be restricted as little as possible by the necessity of covering th m from the attack of the enemy: 4th, in collecting the supplies of the country and storing them in depots, from which they may be dispatched to the bases of operations of the various armies in time to be available for their use."

In modern war "strategical combinations will generally depend for their successful execution upon questions of time. The army which can mobilize, concentrate and strike before the other is ready, can, usually, by keeping up the initiative, push its strategical combinations to a successful issue, one after the other," and the operations of mobilization and concentration belong clearly to logistics.

Strategem, surprise, concealment, subtlety, craftiness are not fundamental and essential elements of strategy and plans which look to these rather than to prudence and sagacity for success, should fail.

In modern war the opening of the campaign follows the declaration so closely that there is no time, as there was formerly, to mature plans. they must be established in peace.

They will consist of "The Plan of War" and "The Project of Operations." The "Plan of War" is dependent, mainly, on the political situation, determines the general conditions which are to govern the war and lies within the province of the government.

The "Project of Operations" is dependent on the plan of war, determines the method of carrying it out and lies within the province of the general in chief.

The general in chief will require information from the government concerning the plan of war as follows

Policy of the government in undertaking war.

The end to be attained.

The ways and means.

This will include information concerning possible friendly or hostile allies, whether the war is to obtain indemnity, to avenge national insult, rectify frontier lines, resist aggressions, &c.: the forces and money available. whether attitude is offensive or defensive· which theatre of operations is preferred from political considerations, &c.*

The project of operations, based on this information, will determine:

The theatre of operations

Choice of a zone of concentration.

The first objectives.

The line of operation.

These will result not only from the plan of war, but also from a consideration of the probable projects of the enemy, the forces which he can place in motion and the lines of operation he is likely to adopt.

It should lead up to the first battle.

The notes which follow will consider these subjects in the order given. They should cover, however briefly, the whole domain of strategy and logistics

---

*"In my judgment the only duty which such a council" (the Aulic council in Vienna) "can safely undertake is that of advising as to the adoption of a general plan of operations. Of course, I do not mean by this a plan which is to embrace the whole course of a campaign, tie down the generals to that course and so inevitably lead to their being beaten I mean a plan which shall determine the objects of a campaign, decide whether offensive or defensive operations shall be undertaken, and fix the amount of material means which may be relied upon in the first instance for the opening of the enterprise, and then for the possible reserves in case of invasion "—Jomini.

II.

THE PLAN OF WAR.—While the plan* of war is dependent on the political situation, determines the general conditions which are to govern and lies within the province of the civil government, its provisions will often hamper the general in chief and it is then clearly his duty to endeavor to modify them. To this extent the plan will lie within his province also.

Extreme instances when projects of operation were greatly modified or neutralized under plans imposed by political considerations may be easily found in the War of Secession. Some of these were due, no doubt, to causes inherent in and inseparable from the form of government, but conditions not altogether dissimilar existed in the Austrian war of 1866, although both belligerents were monarchies supporting large standing armies. In the Franco-German war of 1870, political considerations where they existed at all were thrust into the back ground, at least on the part of the victors, and this contributed so manifestly to victory that in future wars, it seems probable, leaders will be allowed more and more to perfect and carry out their projects unhindered. The reverse will be, as it has always been, a short sighted policy, for success in the field once assured, the civil government will be all-powerful to take what measures it will †

The case of the United States in 1861 is manifestly extreme because the political situation was distinctly abnormal and the conditions unfamiliar and unmanagable. When, later, these became stable and fixed, political and military considerations merged and the conduct of affairs was handed over, not wholly without misgiving, to a single, unhampered leader.

German statesmen, on the contrary, had looked forward for a long time to a war with France, shaping the policy of the government and organizing the nation for offence and defence with this end in view After many years of general compulsory service nearly everyone was a soldier and all of her rulers held high rank in the army or navy· in short, political and dynastic scruples were ignored or compounded, with a steadfast purpose and a forethought which it would be hard to match.

---
*The expression "*Plan* of War" is in a measure confusing but has been retained for want of a better.

†"If there be any sure lession taught by the military experience of nations it is that when extrinsic influences whether from councils, or war offices intrude into the direction of military affairs, all hope of success is gone "—Swinton

Conditions, political or other, favorable to a nation about to engage in war "cannot be created by the genius of a general in chief, but rather by the prudence of governments and by the sacrifices that a people is willing to make Those peoples who recognize the importance of these advantages, will be ever ready to submit to all the expenses which military operations entail. Those who, not understanding it or distracted by preoccupations of another kind, neglect them during peace, may be certain beforehand of condemning their armies to the defensive and their country to invasion."* They will turn, nevertheless, when the crisis has come to whatever armed forces there are, for deliverance and there is no question that, as a soldier, the general-in-chief must accept the charge, no matter how inadequate the means which are provided nor how small allowance is made for the gravity and difficulty of his task. He will have one advantage and only one, he will be in position to demand a free footing as the price of his acceptance, and, this granted, he has obtained a concession of great import. On the other hand if the means furnished him are inadequate and the civil government insists nevertheless on moulding his projects to fit political exigencies, it will be the duty of the general in chief to point out where and how these changes are vicious and, failing to convince, he may refuse the charge with propriety both as soldier and patriot. If he do not he may add another to the list of those who have marched against their better judgment to disaster

But in any case something of compromise on both sides will be expedient. War is a continuation of state policy and soldiers are the servants of the state It is human nature when civil ministers and military leaders are limited, more or less, each by their own horizon, it is the duty of the latter to make converts of the former if they can, urging persistently that the shortest and surest road to all goals lies through the field of battle

Allies.—The question of possible friendly or hostile allies has often complicated if not dictated the conditions which govern a plan of war The coalitions against France begat by the revolution constrained Napoleon to a fierce offensive from the start, if only that his enemies might not join forces afterwards, when France had allies of her own his plans were time and again disturbed by solicitude for them. But Napoleon was, in effect, a military dictator and he had, therefore, the advantage that his designs were never confused by divided responsibility and conflicting

---
*Derrécagaix

England and France were possible and, at one time, probable allies of the Confederates. The United States government was perplexed and harrassed with questions arising from this until late in the war. Their solution reacted often enough on the conduct of active operations, especially on the high seas and in the blockade of the southern coast; not infrequently, it is said, though of course more obscurely, on land.

The prelude to the Austro-Prussian war of 1866 seemed at one time a tangle of calculations referable to the question of allies. The German Confederation, a legacy of the Napoleonic wars, was a league of sovereign states so loosely united that the impending struggle was almost free from the sinister ear-marks of civil war. Still, to the Emperor and King and to the German people it appeared fratricidal and palpably unwise, and both monarchs dreaded a rupture, all the more that public opinion was distinctly hostile. The question of allies was sharply defined at once when Prussia withdrew from the Confederation, because those states which remained became, ipso facto, arrayed against her. Of these the kingdom of Bavaria furnished an army corps to the federal army, Wurtemberg, Baden and Hesse-Darmstadt, together, another, and all of these South-German states were, more or less, in religious, dynastic and political sympathy with Austria. Several states in the north, notably Hanover, were wedged in between the eastern and western provinces of Prussia —most awkwardly for that kingdom,—and Hanover had some admirably trained forces. Saxony, on the south, sided openly with Austria. Together these states could place at least 150,000 soldiers in the field. Hanover endeavored to remain neutral knowing well that on account of geographical position military reasons, if no others, would lead to the occupation of her territory.

Moreover, the course which some of these states would finally take was by no means certain because their rulers strove primarily to preserve a subsequent independence which could be secured only by siding with the victors; while the sympathies of the people were pretty evenly divided. This led to a vacillating course of action not without effect, afterwards, on military operations, and was a factor which the foresight of Bismarck and of his military coadjutor took into account in converting the king who, personally, was very unwilling to take the offensive.

Of the greatest importance, however, to … … … the offensive and defensive alliance which gave Prussia … … the army and navy of Italy, a … … … … Austrian dominion and to complete the unfinished war of 1859. Finally, the armed intervention of France was a contingency which must be provided for as it might incline to the side of one belligerent or the other

Turning to the Franco-German war there is now no doubt that the project of the French emperor was boldly offensive and founded, primarily, on the faith that Austria and perhaps Italy would join hands with him. Then, too, he calculated that the forces of the South-German states if not actively hostile to, would be luke-warm adherents of Prussia, and that, in any event, they would remain in and guard their respective territories.*

It is clear from the foregoing examples how the existence or absence of allies exerts a powerful influence and it should be clear also that this influence predominates in fixing on a belligerent an offensive or defensive attitude

Wars to obtain an indemnity or to rectify frontier lines offer, as such, few considerations of special value. The former if between maritime powers, will often be confined, mainly, to naval operations and both are essentially offensive. The most natural step would be to occupy territory, in one case, especially, the territory in dispute, the object being to hold it for indemnity or to secure its cession.

Sometimes, at a critical phase of strained political relations, some overt act on one side will arouse great popular passion on the other. Mediation will then be inadmissible and it will be idle to argue in the face of just resentment that retaliation is not a lofty code, and unsafe to insinuate that national honor is a quixotic figment. It may be pointed out, however, that in emergencies like this the grievance is clearly on one side only, and that a people inclined to be sensitive should be prepared to chastise a powerful adversary and, if necessary, to seek him beyond the seas under conditions which he himself will be largely able to impose

Available forces.—At first sight it appears easy to make a correct estimate of the armed strength available for war. It is not; and the general must revise the lists which are given him, with great care, if only, for one reason, because civil ministers and the people are always over-sanguine as to numbers and efficiency. "Available" forces are those only which are well drilled and disciplined and which can be assembled at a particular place in a specified time, properly armed, equipped and supplied. Poor

---
*Attention may be called here to the fact which will be discussed further on, that one of the first results of German strategy was to practically denude these states of troops and to lay open their frontier towards France

troops cannot be made available, and to place them guarding communications or in reserve or sandwiched in with good ones, are lame and perilous makeshifts with which no wise leader will delude himself The idea of making some use of them is alluring, but they must be unflinchingly discarded as a worthless encumbrance.

Sometimes generals have been forced to employ untrained or indifferent troops owing to methods against which they protested in vain. During the American civil war Northern generals had often, if not regularly, to accept some troops which formed only weak links in the strength of their lines. A demoralizing system of recruitment, adopted and persistently adhered to for political reasons only, allowed "veteran regiments to dwindle away, while new ones were raised in which all from the colonel down, had to learn their duties together. As a result. the old organizations were often ineffective for want of numerical strength and the new ones inefficient for want of military training "—In one instance a general in command was reinforced by a considerable body of troops so undisciplined and riotous, that he was obliged to employ his seasoned regiments to disarm and guard them. Instances were too common to cause remark where wholly inexperienced men were appointed to high rank and command from civil life; and remonstrances were met in at least one flagrant case with the reply that it would be useless to discuss the matter as the appointment had been made to conciliate certain interests and would in no event be changed.

But the number even of those troops which are known to be efficient must be counted with caution Only those are available for a leader who can help carry out his plans. The Austrian infantry is a gallant force, admirably trained and equipped, but its quality as an instrument of war has been questioned * Its inferiority was due, no doubt, to the variety of races in the ranks, Czechs, Hungarians, Poles, Croats, Italians &c., who, as a rule, could have no heart in any common cause. Large numbers of these surrendered, armed and unwounded, to the Prussians at Sadowa, and this must have convinced the Austrian commander that he should not have counted on their availability

In 1870 the French War Department could show a force on paper of a million men, but of these nearly 500,000. the recently organized Gardes Mobiles. had to be left out of account. A considerable part no one seems to have known how considerable.— were the "reserve" troops. and opinions differ as to how many of

---
*Napoleon spoke of it, somewhat uncivilly, as "la mauvaise infanterie Autrichienne"

these were well trained   After making deductions for the garrisons in Algiers and elsewhere and for an indefinite aggregate of individual soldiers who at the last moment do not respond to the call to arms, the effective force seemed, early in July, to be about 340,000, and Napoleon III calculated that about 250,000, to be followed by an immediate reserve, would be available for a prompt, offensive advance   When, however, in the last days of July, he arrived in Metz, he found less than 200,000 men assembled along the frontier, insufficiently equipped, only partially organized, and wanting the commonest necessities, while the railroads were choked for miles with supplies which could not be distributed.

From the beginning of a campaign other causes are at work which reduce the numbers available for battle, apart from the killed and wounded   The sick, the men on detached service and in the administrative departments—the shirks, stragglers &c , cruelly deplete the ranks. In 1861 McClellan had an army of about 150,000, of these about 8,000 were absent, 10,000 sick and 20,000 on extra duty; and this showing is favorable because no active campaign was then in progress. Later in the war the percentage of men detailed in the supply departments was excessive. "As soon as our regiments arrived at their posts, details began to be made for all the uses of administration,—in the trains, hospitals, headquarters, engineers, telegraph corps, post office, ordnance, clerks, mechanics &c , the greatest of all enemies being the quartermaster's department   The officers at the heads of these departments would by some means learn the names of the best men and these would be detailed, sometimes reducing regiments of 1,000 to 3 or 400, with a full complement of officers, the detailed majority representing the best men who gave tone to all the rest "* In the army of the Cumberland about 22,000 men, or about 17 per-cent were on extra duty or detached service and were sorely missed at Chickamauga. These details were, it is true, altogether extravagant and, in number, far beyond what would have been required with specially recruited and instructed non-combatants such as exist in modern European armies   "The loss in strength owing to disease is scarcely credible " * * * "It is something horrible to see day after day whole railway trains full of sick being transported to the rear, reserves only slowly coming in, and no remedy available for putting an end to this continuous process of destruction. The conditions of health obtaining in the German army in France were quite favorable; no dangerous pestilence broke out; and yet during the

---
*Hazen.

course of the war 400,000 sick, besides the 100,000 wounded, were obliged to have recourse to the hospitals. The average duration of their absence was about 20 days· the total result, in respect to martial achievements, is accordingly equivalent to the absence of twelve army corps for three weeks.* Including losses in battle "a battalion which at the commencement of the campaign, numbers 1,000 rifles, sinks at the close to 300 The army corps, in respect of the number of their combatants, become weak divisions, the divisions weak brigades And yet a definite plan and definite demands upon them are inseparable from their names "

With regular troops, straggling on the march will be usually checked by the company officers, but in a large army of volunteers there will be here and there regiments which will furnish their full quota of stragglers; and stringent orders will be necessary, together with a provost guard, to enforce them. For an army corps a well disciplined battalion or a regiment reduced in numbers should be detailed for this purpose, with a few cavalry to pursue distant men. One or two medical officers attached to the guard will be very useful in detecting malingerers among those numerous stragglers who drift towards the ambulances or hang about the train.†

Skulking in battle is not peculiar to volunteer troops only. in any case it is hard to control because there are many opportunities in action to withdraw from the fight on one pretext or another. With the so-called dispersed or extended order of fighting there is no need for any one to go forward who does not relish his job The Germans, whose fine discipline everyone concedes, have been keen to ferret out, and frank in discussing, their own short comings, and one of them has described what he saw, bearing on this, in battle in 1870—71. "The field was literally strewed with men who had left the ranks and were doing nothing Whole battalions could have been formed from them. From where we stood we could count hundreds. Some were lying down, their rifles pointing to the front, as if they were still in the firing line, and were expecting the enemy to attack them

---

*von der Goltz.
†During the War of Secession the long and forced marches in the interior of the Gulf States developed a class of foragers who deteriorated into marauders of the worst sort They were known as ' bummers,'' and it has been customary to refer to them indulgently if not jocosely, and even to ascribe to them some utility in the way of scouts and flankers Nothing could be more uncandid and no inference more vicious. Their presence with or near the column was unconditionally demoralizing and without a single compensating feature They were, often enough, villanous ruffians whose track was marked by infamous crimes and they easily avoided retribution in part because the prospect of a speedy end to the war seemed to render severe measures of discipline generally undesirable Had the war lasted longer it would have become necessary to stamp them out like fire

at any moment These had evidently remained behind lying down when the more courageous had advanced Others had squatted like hares in the furrows Wherever a bush or ditch gave shelter, there were men to be seen, who in some cases had made themselves very comfortable." * * * "During our advance, before we came under any really serious fire, and while only the whistle of an occasional stray bullet could be heard, we saw six men, one behind the other in a long cue, cowering at the back of a tree. Afterwards I saw this sight so often that I became accustomed to it Who did not? At the time it was new to me. In this instance the sixth was a sergeant." * * * "This epidemic of withdrawing from battle begins with the game and spreading with pestilential rapidity rages over the battlefield like a fever."*

The offensive and defensive.—Whether the attitude of the power about to engage in war shall be offensive or defensive is determined by the plan of war and, therefore, by considerations which either lie beyond the province of the soldier or which he cannot alter In the first case these considerations will be purely political and questions arising from them must be decided, rightly or wrongly, by statesmen.† In the second case the relative situation and conformation of frontiers and the relative state of preparation for war will or will not preclude the offensive. These are clearly conditions which neither the soldier nor anyone can then control.

It is absurd to suppose that a people geographically well placed, with ample strength and means and with a highly organized army, will be content to forego these advantages by a policy of inaction. When both belligerents are equal in these respects or the inequality is not glaring, both will assume the offensive. In other words, political considerations, unfavorable geographical conditions, and weakness, may impose the defensive, but it is illogical to hold that this attitude will ever be taken from choice. Aggressive action is the fundamental attribute of war

Now it has happened very often that a nation has been constrained to await attack from one or more of these causes and to them may be added others, especially in earlier times, where one power has been "caught napping," so to speak, and overrun by another. In modern war the difference of a few days or even of

---

*There was little skulking in battle during the War of Secession, if the writer may generalize . . . ation This was, of course, limited but it extended to troops from . . . armies Situations like those described would have been inco . . . a been due in part, to tactics which kept every soldier from first . . . at least one officer

†Haply t . . . . . t . . . t ey are rare Louvois, Pitt, Carnot Stein, Stanton, Bismarck History has but a short list of them

a few hours in preparation will force the defensive on an unready antagonist, who will then appear to take it from choice. Indeed he may be willing, for it will be easy, to deceive himself in this respect. With no other foundation, and also because belligerents are never so evenly matched in skill or resources that one or the other is not soon obliged to subordinate his plans to those of his adversary, there came a conception of war which divides it, broadly, into offensive and defensive war, into two kinds of war, as it were, different in nature and methods. This difference has been discussed in many solemn chapters which, he will be relieved to know, the student need not read. It will be instructive, nevertheless, to look at the subject from the text-writer's standpoint, to understand why they have devised two forms of war each with its own demands. In doing so it is convenient to imagine relative advantages which each form may have.

Historical offensive &c —Some of the fairest writers have concluded that there is an "historical" offensive and defensive which precedes the strategical. In accord with this, they say, Turkey adopted in 1877 a defensive attitude from the first "because she had entered upon a stage of historical development in which the defensive was alone possible, whilst Russia, driven violently forward by the idea of Panslavism, was naturally forced to attack." From this is concluded that "even before the war, the historical standpoint dictates to the belligerent the manner in which he must wage the war." Surely, this is only a learned way of saying that a nation, for reasons which are or are not historical, may be in a positon where it is her interest to let well enough alone but it is not clear why, if attacked, she should therefore confine herself simply to resistance. In 1877 Turkey had forseen the war which then broke out and was either prepared for it or was not. If prepared, there seems to be no reason why active offensive operations would not have been as gainful for her as for Russia, if not prepared, any other reason given for her defensive attitude is far-fetched

In 1861 the attitude of the Southern States, historically, was certainly defensive. They asked for nothing more than to be let alone, to be allowed to go their own way unhindered. In the light of the four years of war which followed it is doubtful whether under any circumstances they would have gained independence, but they threw away their best chances of success, singularly enough, by first beginning the war and then by allowing the North to organize and perfect her armed forces at leisure. By seizing on military posts and dock yards and, finally, by firing on Fort Sumter the South exasperated and roused the North, alienated the strong public opinion in her favor which existed in that section and put herself in the wrong There was a chance, and not a bad chance, that the slave states would not be interferred with in establishing a new nation,—in any event there could be no harm in inaction for it would give them additional time to prepare for war. The war fairly begun and afterwards at intervals during its progress a vigorous offensive was strongly urged on the Confederate government by some of its best men To many of them this course seemed obvious at first only, a few continued in the belief, at any time throughout the war, that the South could win only by persistent attack. Immediately after the first Federal defeat at Bull Run they contended that the victory should result in the dispersion of all the enemy's forces south of Baltimore, the capture of Washington, and the occupation of Maryland, with the accession of that state to the Southern cause and they pointed out with much force that from these achievements others would continue to flow, as in war one success makes another easier. Moreover, they said, it would be folly to allow McClellan to organize and discipline at leisure the powerful army that in the end wore out the South All this was to be done after freely giving up all other points, concentrating in Virginia, and thus obtaining the full benefit of interior lines General Beauregard states the case forcibly as follows "Apart from an active material ally, a country in fatal war must depend upon the vigor of its warfare, the more inferior the country, the bolder and more enterprising the use of the resources, especially if its frontiers are convenient to the enemy. I was convinced that our success lay in a short, quick war of decisive blows, before the Federals, with their vast resources, could build up a great military power, to which end a concerted use of our forces, immediate and sustained, was necessary, so that, weaker though we were at all separate points, we might nevertheless strike with superior strength at some chosen decisive point, and after victory there reach for victory now made easier elsewhere, and thus sum up success Instead of this, which in war we call concentration, our actual policy was diffusion, an inferior Confederate force at each separate point defensively confronting a superior Federal force, our power daily shrinking, that of the enemy increasing " * * * "About three months after the battle of Manassas I proposed that the army should be raised to an effective of 60,000 men, by drawing 20,000 for the immediate enterprise from several points along the seaboard, not even then threatened, and from our advanced position be swiftly thrown across the Potomac at a point which I had carefully surveyed for that purpose and move upon the rear of Washington, thus forcing McClellan to a decisive engagement before his organization was completed, and while our own army had the advantage of discipline and prestige This plan, approved by General Gustavus W. Smith as well as by General Johnston, was submitted to Mr Davis, but rejected because he would not venture to strip those points of the troops we required Even if those points had been captured, though none were even then threatened, they must have reverted as a direct consequence to so decided a success I was willing, then, should it come to that, to exchange even Richmond temporarily for Washington. Yet it was precisely from similar combinations and elements that the army was made up, to enable it the next spring, under General Lee, to encounter McClellan at the very door of Richmond If that which was accepted as a last defensive resort against an overwhelming aggressive army had been used in an enterprising offensive against that same army while yet in the raw, the same venture had been made at less general risk, less cost of valuable lives, and with greater certain results. The Federal army would have had no chance meanwhile to become tempered to that magnificent military machine which, through all its defeats and losses, remained sound, and was stronger, with its regular assimilated new strength, at the end of the war than ever before, the pressure would have been lifted from Kentucky and Missouri and we should have maintained an active defensive warfare, that is, should have taken and kept the offensive against the enemy, enforcing peace." Later in the war General Beauregard "urged particularly that our warfare was sure of final defeat unless we attempted decisive strokes that might be followed up to the end, and that, even if earlier defeat might chance from the risk involved in the execution of the necessary combinations, we ought to take that risk and thereby either win or end an otherwise useless struggle "

Strategical and tactical offensive &c —The reader who follows ever so many discussions of the strategical and tactical offensive and defensive may be alternately persuaded, but in the end he will find himself between the devil and the deep sea A distinction between them is so obvious that, to begin with, no other definition is called for. To say, e. g. that strategical consists in repelling on a great scale the attack in the position we have chosen step towards obscuring what is plain. After a first step critical inquiry gains ground easily: in this case it seeks to establish a connection and to show that the strategical offensive is practicable only when combined with the tactical and that they belong inseparably together, the same being true of both species of defensive This is the conviction of at least one writer of note, and it is a clean-cut, attractive theory which seems to promise solid ground for further progress It is disappointing, therefore, to find that he begs the question "It is the tactical attack," he says, "that first lends energy to the strategical, completes and finishes it with results. The strategical sows the seed, the tactical reaps the harvest. The weakliest opponent, too, who is strategically driven into a corner, will appeal to the fortune of arms upon the field, before declaring himself vanquished. If the attacker were to stop here, in order in this last crisis to enjoy the advantages of the defence, it would be very frequently tantamount to renouncing his claim to decide the struggle; for the enemy; who, up to then has been the repelling and expectant party, will also remain so to the last hour; and all the more readily, too, seeing that his prospects are, as a rule, not improved by it " "It is similar with the strategical and tactical defensive He who has acted in his movements on the defensive, will, in most cases, observe a repelling attitude upon the battle-field. The attacker presses him, he relinquishes advancing operations in favor of action. And there it is exceedingly difficult for the defender to find the right moment for shaking off the yoke imposed upon him, in order, in turn, to play hammer, and not anvil. Here is seen what is imported when one party has learnt to consider itself domineered over by another. Even with superior numbers on its side, it will often remain on the defensiue, and be glad if it can remain so to the end with any degree of comfort." "When the original defence is due to the constraining necessity, the army will usually remain on the defensive. If the enemy's attack has been repulsed, only in rare cases will all doubts have been dispelled as to whether he will not again return with renewed strength and energy. or whether his repulse was final and complete. Great precautions will almost always have to be taken so as not, by a too rapid advance, to risk a success which has been already achieved. The defender will be content to hold his position, so as not to lose what is certainly his He will readily abandon all idea of adding to his successes. because he has, as it is, a victory in his hands. And then it is never at the moment felt to be quite certain that the attacker has relaxed his efforts."

As a matter of fact, no connection exists inherently between the strategical and tactical offensive and defensive, and the foregoing argument taken from a book which is often quoted and widely read,* establishes none. Indeed others have maintained with greater reason that it should be profitable to combine the offensive with the defensive by taking the initiative in movement and then forcing an antagonist to become the assailant. The student, however, may well be discouraged to read that this combination is "very difficult to realize, and scarcely ever to be met with in military history." Others, again, have endeavored to show that defensive strategy with defensive tactics, adhered to throughout, all else being equal, should succeed.

A short general discussion of the subject should rid it of ambiguity it is involved only for those who are captivated by a theory and attempt to pursue it to some end.

The two forms compared.—1st. It has been claimed for the assailant that at the outset and for an indeterminate time afterwards, he has the advantage because he is carrying out definite plans. He should therefore, be able to forsee and to provide against the steps which the enemy may take to thwart him, with the additional chance that the enemy working in the dark, may not take them. This should lead to a first success and that again to others, until the defender is compelled to follow the lead of his adversary.

2nd. The second claim for the so-called offensive is based on considerations which are purely psychological and in the same breath asserts that, and explains why, all the triumphs are on its side. The attack appeals to intellectual and moral forces and these are stimulated again and again to effort by the demands of changing situations. it requires and produces energy. "A spirit of enterprise is aroused' and communicated to all, even to the lowest. Subordinate commanders are on their mettle and vie with each other in seeking opportunity for action, each in his own sphere.

3rd. Finally, it is stated, as in a nut-shell, that the great difference between the two forms lies in the fact that the defence, to succeed, must do so at all points, while the assailant is victorious if he gain the advantage anywhere.

It is noticable that while the so called offensive claims with confidence "all the triumphs" for its own, the reasons advanced for results so important, are intangibl   the advocates of the defensive on the c h.   gue

---
* "The Nation in arms " von der Goltz.

clearly in its favor, and while their reasoning is to a certain extent negative it is none the less sound, and anyone may understand it. It affirms.

1st. That the defensive is first and foremost simple while the difficulties of the assailant increase with each step forward.

2nd. The offensive claims that there are always several or many points of irruption all of which the defence must observe but that anyone of them is open to the full force of attack. This is not true. The points of possible irruption are, as a rule, very few in number, they may be and, in the case of military nations, they are, reduced to a minimum. How many of these an enemy may use can be predicated long in advance and to a vigilant defence it should be clear which of them he is about to take in ample time to frustrate his plans. It is not the case of a river, notoriously an ineffective barrier, because it can be crossed anywhere it is the case of a military frontier, corresponding roughly to natural boundary lines.

3rd. The army on the defensive is easily supplied, it is in the midst of its magazines or can fall back to them. To feed it with men and material is hardly a problem, and its losses from straggling, desertion and sickness are comparatively very small. Surrounded by a friendly people and at home, it has the incentive of defending its own. On the other hand the invader must bring up his supplies of all kinds along a vulnerable line which he is obliged to guard at a great sacrifice of men, and back along this line there is a constant stream of sick and wounded and of empty wagons. The difficulties due to this increase enormously with the advance until the latter reaches its utmost limits,—unless, indeed, victory has declared decisively for the invader and he has been able to annex and hold with a great reserve force, the country in his rear

It is only necessary to cite some of the examples from wars, with which the partisan of one or the other forms endeavors to prove his case, to be convinced that there is something fundamentally forced and unreal in his assumptions. Any unbiased person who reads an account of the campaign of 1866 will conclude that the Prussians won, not because of any "living force which dwells in the attack," but because they were well led and had breech-loading rifles· and that the Austrians lost not from being on the defensive, but because they were badly led and because they loaded from the muzzle. Indeed it is very easy to show that Benedek should have been the victor in spite of inferior weapons, and then the fine, Austrian cavalry which saved h s army would, in pursuit, have debited the "offensive" with at least one undoubted disaster of the first order. Again, what can be said of arguments and views, which by any possibility can lead a distinguished author to the following conclusion "From reverses at first, material strength may—when a proud and strong nation is at its back—accrue to the defence The Northern States during the great rebellion, and France in the second half of the last war, furnish remarkable instances."

To follow the subject further would be to thrust considerations upon the student which, as has been claimed, he need not read. It is treated by all writers on the lines indicated in the foregoing summary,—by most of them with an earnestness which it does not deserve.

Conclusions.—In the conclusions which follow, the terms "offensive" and "defensive" are retained because they are indigenous to military phraseology and it is difficult to elude them

1. When war is brewing between two powers one of them will, as a rule, take the initiative in preparing for it. From this time until the war is ended that power may continue to act offensively, even under defeat; or it may at any moment await the adversary's movements and act on the defensive, even in victory. Either attitude may be imposed by the soundest resoning and be the best which can be taken under the circumstances.

2. When two belligerents are equally well prepared, it may still be altogether judicious for one of them to choose the defensive His chances of success will then be at least as good as those of his adversary.

3 History shows no preponderance of advantage to either one form or the other. If it be true that the offensive is credited with the greater number of victories it is because it was better prepared and better led in each case

4 However equally well prepared both belligerents may seem to be, one is usually assured of his own superiority in advance or else he discovers it very soon. If it be great, and, as a rule, it is, he will push forward with vigor and the other is doomed to defeat.

5. In the history of wars this marked superiority of one or the other of two apparently equal combatants is very common and very curious. The theory of an offensive and defensive form of war is a handy but far-fetched explanation. It is not due to these it is due to superior leadership on one or the

other side, and to this only. Between two leaders any inequality, however small, is for all practical purposes infinite. Whether the inferior miss his goal by an inch or a mile, it is enough that he misses it.

III.

PROJECTS OR OPERATION —If strategy selects and occupies the theatre of operations, these reciprocal functions will be directly affected by the size of armies. As armies grow larger difficulties thicken rapidly.

For this reason war in the future must lose much of the mobility of former campaigns. "The masses of the future will preclude tours de force and requirements of transport and supply will compel the adoption of the simplest plans."

The principles of strategy which will underlie these plans are simple also·

1 Operate by interior lines.

2 Operate upon the enemy's communications without exposing your own.

These truisms sum up everything included by writer after writer in "the great principles of strategy which remain unchanged." The first should enable a belligerent to concentrate the largest possible force on any desirable point at the right time and should, therefore, enable him to engage superior with inferior forces. The second should compel an adversary to retreat, to change his base, or to form front to a flank.

Both principles have lost much of their significance. The modern weapon is so huge—10 or 12 or more army corps—that it must be wielded with both hands with no thought of feint or finesse. Where, formerly, small states and communities of wavering allegiance interposed an indefinite frontier, political boundary lines are now sharply defined, and behind them stretch in all directions perfected roads and railways into rich provinces and fields of supply. It will not be possible to operate against these lines of communication so broadly as to break up the organic efficiency of the hosts which they sustain, and movements against them will be dictated, more and more, by tactical considerations Movements of this kind will be strategic in their nature and may be vital in results; but it will be quite impossible to forsee and provide for the situations which call for them, in any general strategic plan.

With pencil and paper the advantages of interior lines are, geometrically, very striking, nor have they been unreal in deciding campaigns and wars. But this has always been due rather to nicely timed and rapid movements together with superior preparation and fine leading. To-day the telegraph connects armies and parts of armies with each other and all with the highest in command and the latter is within wide limits, independent of time and space. Moreover, most nations have sought and, in a measure, obtained political boundary lines which narrow the possibility of favorable conditions of attack and, where necessary, have supplemented these by the establishment of military frontiers. With term after term eliminated there will be few chances for combinations and the problem confronting the leader, from its very nakedness, will be profoundly difficult

A new complication in war will be inseparable it seems, in the leading of great masses of troops. These will spread over a front so wide that the opportunity for favorable if not decisive tactical action will arise at this or that point when there will be no chance to first obtain consent, and the subordinate commander of any considerable body of troops will not only seize it, but the necessity for doing so will be in a measure thrust upon him. It is doubtful whether independent action of this kind can be prevented and, if it can, whether prevention will be advisable.

Whoever reads the story of the Franco-German war will be struck by the fact that many battles were brought on by comparatively small bodies and that (notably at Worth) orders from higher authority to suspend the action were met with the reply that *it was no longer possible to do so.* Indeed all the battles up to Gravelotte-St. Privat were brought on in a manner and at times and places not contemplated by the supreme command and clearly beyond its control; yet, from the results of these battles, the strategical features of the war developed almost from day to day. They were not accidental collisions—as they have been called—on the contrary, they were in every case due to the deliberate action of subordinate leaders followed up with all the confidence and deliberation of design. Their action was accepted, at all events tacitly, at the general headquarters, but in the orders for subsequent movements which each battle called forth there is a non-committal silence regarding it which denotes uneasiness and concern. In the German official report the question is handled with gloves.

The battle of Borny is a well known example, where v. d. Goltz with an advance-guard brigade, bodly attacked a French corps deployed and covering the withdrawal across the Moselle of the French army. It is not clear that he had any well defined strategic object whatever, since the explanation that he wished to delay the retreat and also prevent a flank movement against the troops to his left, has all the signs of an afterthought. It is very clear, however, that the strategic results were exceedingly important, for, assuming that the retreat had been delayed, the German headquarters promptly ordered a "vigorous offensive by the II army" towards the roads west of Metz.

The explanation of this gallant leader of gallant troops adds nothing to the merit of his course nor would the absence of explanation detract from it. "It was their high spirit, their high training, their knowledge of war, which made the German leaders so hard to keep within the leash when they saw the prey before them and realized that it was a matter of moments whether it could be seized or not."

That in case of failure they would have been blamed is probably true but means very little. Battles and campaigns have often been lost or won, since war began, by the bungling or expert initiative of subordinates. There is nothing novel in the situation. What is novel is the matter-of-course high spirit, high training and knowledge of war which prevailed and which led commanders, from the highest to the lowest, to perceive, whether dimly or not, the common design and that a certain course of action would advance it. This is war—this has always been war the difference is only in this, that while in the past, independent initiative was possible, in the future it will be inevitable and must be prepared for but no preparation will avail except constant and most industrious training.

Theatre of operations Selection. If—again—strategy selects and occupies the theatre of operations it is plain that a correct choice is all important. But in modern war the scope for selection is greatly curtailed. This is due, primarily, to the fact that the consolidation of nationalities, for which the peoples were struggling more or less blindly in the 18th century, has now at the end of the 19th been well nigh accomplished and the power of resistance enormously increased. As has been pointed out, frontier lines have been rectified and military frontiers established. These are often guarded at places favorable for ingress by vast fortified camps; indeed a military power is not unlike a huge fortress in which, thanks to general compulsory service, every able-bodied man is a soldier and which an adversary may reconnoiter for a long time without finding a suitable point for attack.

When Bonaparte attacked the Austrians in 1796, he could select Italy as a theatre because at that time a score or more of petty, independent states. One of these, Piedmont, could be isolated by the direction of his advance and crushed from the coalition; while along the northern frontier, like a great traverse, stretched the neutral mountains of Switzerland The first successes were followed promptly by the establishment of a new, fortified, military base, and, later, by supreme efforts to oppose a national frontier to Austria by organizing a great, Italian republic.

In 1799 Austria was foremost in joining the coalition, not with the ambition of regaining her possessions in Italy but because "the safety of the Austrian monarchy imposed on her the duty of rescuing Germany from the danger threatened by the estabment of the French at the gates of the Voralberg."

In 1800, the plan of the campaign of Marengo was based on the fact that Switzerland, no longer neutral, was now in possession of the French and enabled them "to take in reverse the enemy's lines of operation in Italy "

In 1805 the Austrians violated without scruple the territory of Bavaria, expecting thereby to force the Elector to join the coalition and to carry the theatre of war to the Rhine. By doing this they increased their distance from the Russians, and by pushing on to Ulm enabled Napoleon to base on the situation his plan of a campaign which ended at Austerlitz.

These are all elementary considerations—but whoever leaves them out, attracted by more conspicuous and dramatic features of Napoleon's campaigns, will miss the first chapter.

It is clear, then, why the scope for selection of a theatre was formerly much wider than it is now and than it will be in the future; at least as between nations with large standing armies Every first class power, excepting the United States, is armed, while the integrity of the smaller and weaker European States is guaranteed by international agreement or by other conditions which are, perhaps, more effective. The integrity of Belgium was guaranteed in 1839, Great Britain agreeing to cooperate against the nation violating her neutrality. yet the Belgian people have been greatly concerned lest in case of war between Germany and France one or the other power would, from necessity, operate through their territory, and they have, therefore, fortified. and are prepared to hold, the line of the Maas.

The integrity of Switzerland was guaranteed in 1815 That her territory will not be violated in war is due to a number of reasons, not the least weighty of them being due to disadvantages o   a course from a military standpoint

The F..n.. German frontier is, therefore, about 200 miles long It has been covered on the side of France "with a net-work, nay, a breast-plate of forts and fortified places," presenting but few gaps, and the presence of these easily explained by military considerations. The French have almost solved the problem of barring all the roads by which an enemy coming from the east or the north-east might attempt to enter the country.

In an unarmed power like the United States it would seem that conditions would be in sharp contrast to those which have been developed in Europe. But however great her degree of immunity from the danger of war may be it is not complete, and when war comes she will be confronted by limitations more hard and fast than military frontiers and fortresses. A nation which is obliged at the last moment to raise, drill, equip and supply new levies,—to obstruct channels of approach by sea, and, perhaps, to control or suppress domestic violence at the same time, will not be embarrassed by having to select a theatre of operations.

Military geography.—In general, a good knowledge of the geography of the country and good maps are indispensible. To be available at any time, geographical and statistical information should be collected during peace by officers specially assigned to that duty, published in comprehensive and handy form and held ready for use It is difficult to place limits on the amount and kinds of information which should be gathered, for it is probably true enough that the most common-place fact may be of possible service to the general. In practice, however, he will be able to use very little,* but it is all important that the information which he requires be both complete and exact. Obscure points of geography, cavalry or wheelmen or countrymen and spies will clear up for him. The available maps of most civilized countries are very good, some of them are excellent and there are innumerable volumns of statistics. Maps and tables of statistical information specially compiled for use in the field will be immensely valuable, but the former must be clear and free from confusing detail. Some European maps, notably German, are remarkable examples of cartographic art, but it is burdensome to use them and indications are not wanting, that in the war with France some of them were defective.

If specially prepared maps and tables are not forthcoming, everything necessary can be usually made up by intelligent staff officers in a comparatively short time. If a country is a terra incognita the general must obtain his in   an

---

*It is difficult to read without impatience quibbous like   of a wholesome herb may involve the failing   ure point of geography the success of a campaign "

and from day to day if it is not, it will be easy to ascertain, e. g., whether its roads be good or bad and how and when they are wanting,—and this without a knowledge of geology.* Certainly it will be much the best way, to have all necessary data gathered in advance by officers who know what is wanted and will become expert at the work; but it is not wise to exalt their occupation into a special branch of military science with which officers generally should be familiar. The study of geography, whether it be called "military geography" or not, will not help to confer what is known as a good eye for terrain or coup d'oeil.

Emergency reports.—During the War of Secession portions of the country which were practically unknown to Northern leaders became possible theatres of operations and it was necessary to obtain information concerning them on the spot, as it were, with the aid of staff officers. One of innumerable, excellent reports of this kind was made to the commanding general, Department of the Gulf, in January 1864, by an Aid de Camp,† concerning the routes from the Mississippi River to the interior of Texas. It is quoted here, considerably curtailed, as a model of what may be called emergency reports. After giving the distances from a number of points on the Mississippi and in Arkansas to Shreveport, La., and from there to Houston, Texas, the writer continues

"The water via Red River commences falling about the 1st of May, and the navigation of the river for the most of our gunboats and transports is not reliable after that time. The months of March and April are unfavorable for operations in Northern and Eastern Texas, owing to the high stage of water in the Sabine, Néches, and Trinity Rivers and their tributaries, and the overflows to which their banks are subject. The concentration of all the forces available for operations west of the Mississippi in the vicinity of Shreveport requires that the line of supply with the Mississippi be kept up. It would not be practicable to abandon the base with so large a force, with a line of operations of 300 miles, through a country occupied by the enemy, to be overcome before communication could possibly be effected with points held by us on the coast."

"The water communication to Alexandria cannot be depended on after the 1st of May, and it would be necessary to depend on the road from Natchez, a distance of 80 miles, or possibly from Harrisonburg, a distance of 50 miles. Boats of very light

---

*In the Program of Instruction of the Artillery School for 1882, geology, subdivided into five sections appears as an adjunct to military geography, as part of the course of study. It has since been dropped.

†Major D C Houston, U S A

draught, say 3 or 3½ feet of water, may go to Alexandria during low water at ordinary seasons, but the large majority of our boats and gun-boats are of greater draught than this The most reliable routes would be by the railroad from Vicksburg to Shreveport The track is now laid from Vicksburg to Monroe. The road, is graded from Monroe to Shreveport, and mostly bridged, the distance is 96 miles. There is a good wagon road from Monroe to Shreveport, crossing the Washita River and other streams.'

"It would require at least three months to rebuild this railroad, which is indispensible to the supply of an army in Northeastern Texas."

"Suppose it is determined to concentrate the forces near Shreveport, preliminary to a movement into Texas. This point is the principal depot of the enemy west of the Mississippi. There are some machine-shops and dock-yards there and the place is fortified by a line of works with a radius of 2 or 3 miles. The position is a strong one, being on a bluff and commanding the eastern bank "

"The most direct and only reliable line of supply to this point would be the road from Vicksburg to Shreveport, railroad as far as Monroe, 52 miles, and a graded road the rest of the way, 96 miles. It would be necessary to put the road in running order and procure materials for completing the road. This line could be held much more easily than the Red River, which is very narrow and crooked and which has, in many places, high bluff banks where field artillery could be placed to enfilade the channel and have no fear of gun-boats Such a point is Grand Ecore, where the bluff is 120 feet high. This point, I have been informed by spies, is fortified."

"Suppose our forces to be united at Shreveport, which could probably be effected during the season of high water, and that arrangements have been perfected to supply the army by the road from Vicksburg via Monroe, Arkansas and Louisiana clear of rebels, and the enemy in retreat. Whatever way he takes we must follow and expect to have our path disputed at every point, as he will be driven to desperate efforts. The numerous streams with high banks will afford him a favorable opportunity to retard our progress and effect a secure retreat to any point he may select. Our subsequent movements cannot well be foreseen. It does not seem probable that the enemy will return to Houston unless his force is large and he should propose to draw us in to a t"

"Again, recurring to the line of supply, it will be seen that the Vicksburg and Shreveport road extends to Marshall, where there is an interval of 40 miles to Henderson, whence the road is completed to Galveston. The road from Marshall to Henderson, however, is graded, and could be completed in a short time. In case the enemy should abandon the coast this road will fall into our possession, and supplies could be obtained from two directions. Our colored troops, who are especially qualified for fighting guerrillas, could be usefully employed in guarding the entire line of this road from Vicksburg to Galveston Texas is said to be full of blacks, who will be a valuable auxiliary in our operations in that State."

"I should estimate, roughly, that it would require until some time in May to effect the union of forces and be prepared with transportation for a movement into the interior. This would be about the commencement of the season most favorable for active operations in Texas I suppose by that time wagon trains will be provided to haul supplies from Monroe to Shreveport, that the railroad will be in running order to Monroe, and the work of completing the road well under way."

"A movement by the coast of Texas possesses great advantages. Our troops and supplies can be quickly moved by steamer to any point on the coast. Landings can be threatened at different points and the enemy kept in ignorance of our intentions. We now hold the harbor of Matagorda, the best on the coast, next to Galveston. We have a secure point for the debarkation of troops and supplies. The distance by land to Houston is 150 miles, over good roads, three in number, one via Texana and Wharton, one via Matagorda and Columbia, and the third along the beach to the mouth of Brazos River."

"Very little baggage need be required on this march, as the point of supply can be transferred to Brazos River and San Luis Pass in succession. A much less force would be required for this operation than the other. The rebel forces now in Arkansas will remain there as long as our force is opposed to them, and we would only have to meet the force in lower Texas."

It is evident from the foregoing example how, even in case of a sparsely settled and new country uncontrolled by frontiers or fortresses, the influence of railway lines predominates. Together with the ··· of armies and the facility with which information is obtained ··· are the prime influences which have modified strategy. The study of military geography today is largely a study of lines of communication, and these are fixed by railways.

The military geography of Canada presents the case of a region in which, so far as it is a military objective, old and settled conditions prevail, but without an organized system of defense. The information which follows was obtained from sources open to anyone and easily accessible. it is given here condensed as much as possible.

Extent. Of Canada's 3,500,000 square miles only about one tenth is settled. The rest is, more or less, an unexplored and unknown wilderness. The settled portion comprises the provinces which lie north and east of the great lakes and extend to the Atlantic For military purposes this is the only important section excepting the south-western portion of the Pacific province which includes Vancouver Island and in which lies the terminus of the Pacific railway.

Climate. The cold in winter is severe and the summers are, very warm Sudden changes in temperature are common. Military operations on a large scale are impossible in winter and must be confined to about six months in the year. As far as climatic influences affect the health of troops, it should be good

Population. About 5,000,000. Of these the older settled provinces contain 4,646,000, Ontario alone having over 2,000,000 and Quebec nearly 1,500,000. The center of population lies somewhere in the region north of New York and east of Maine. About 1,000,000 are available for active military service From their ancestry, their mode of life and their habits no better material for soldiers can be found anywhere

Military forces. 35,000 volunteer militia, well organized, armed and equipped. Of these 2000 are cavalry, 1200 field artillery, 2000 garrison artillery and 28,500 infantry. The bulk of these troops are at home in Ontario and Quebec, roughly speaking, by battalions in the large places along the Lakes and the St. Lawrence from Lake Erie east. About one half are drilled and disciplined, but unevenly, some battalions maintaining a high standard and others being inefficient if judged by professional rules. The 18 field-batteries are still armed with 9 pounder, muzzle-loading guns. The infantry is replacing, very slowly, the Snider rifle with the small caliber, Martini-Metford. Supply departments fail altogether and there is no large arsenals or factories. There is an enrolled reserve of a[illegible] men who are supposed to receive a few days training an[illegible]

In studying the military resources of a possible enemy it is not safe to dwell on defects, and it is wise to employ a factor of safety in estimating the resistance which any community may be able to offer. It is reasonable to assume that, if unhindered, Canada could place 100,000 armed men in the field, brave and hardy, organized and equipped, in six weeks, and that a sufficient supply-service would be improvised. Given a leader with brains and resolution this force might add another to the list of surprises which the history of war offers.

Productions. From causes which spring from her institutions, from political conditions and from sparseness of population, Canada, in an economic sense, is a poor country The individual Canadian, however, demands and perhaps requires material comforts in profusion, and these are furnished him bountifully by soil and climate with a large surplus for export. The imports for consumption exceed, in value, the exports. The supply of food, horses and coal is ample for home military purposes, but no invading force could live upon the country even if advancing from day to day and in the most thickly settled parts.

Cities. Leaving out Winnipeg in Manitoba and the places on or near the Atlantic or Pacific coasts there are from 20 to 25 towns of 10,000 inhabitants and over. A straight line drawn from Detroit to Quebec will pass near nearly all of them and they occupy, therefore, a narrow strip of country never further than a few day's march from the frontier. Including Toronto, about two thirds of these places are west of Lake Ontario and lie near together in the cul de sac between that lake and Huron. Montreal is the commercial metropolis with over 216,000 inhabitants, Toronto next with 180,000. Quebec is a shipping port with a population of 63,000, extensive dockyards and water for the largest vessels. Ottawa (45,000) is the political capital. Hamilton (50,000) and Kingston (20,000) complete the list of interior towns of 20,000 and over, Winnipeg (25,000) alone excepted.

Waters. Of the innumerable waters of Canada only the Great Lakes, the St. Lawrence River and the canals apply to this discussion. The Great Lakes are unique geographical features well known in their general character. Lake Michigan alone lies wholly within the United States while the Canadian shore line of the others has about twice the extent of its neighbor's. Vessels of the largest size can sail between certain lake ports, but owing to the canals and the river above Montreal, only vessels of a limited draft can make a continuous voyage from any Lake port to the o．．．．an and for only six months in the year The straits which connect Superior, Huron, Erie and Ontario in the order mentioned, are narrow channels forming in each case part of the boundry line between the two countries and commanded throughout their length by the shores of both.

The St. Lawrence River from Kingston forms for over 100 miles the boundary line of the state of New York, and from Kingston to Montreal it interposes between the most populous parts of the Dominion. It is navigable, with occasional interruptions, by sea going vessels to Montreal. At Quebec it widens to 5 or 6 miles and from there to the sea it is, essentially, a great bay not unlike the Chesapeake in extent. Of the tributaries of the St. Lawrence only one, the Richelieu, is of importance, as the outlet of Lake Champlain. It is navigable by means of a dam and lock and other improvements from the St. Lawrence to the lake, a distance of 80 miles, the total water distance between Montreal and New York being 450. Above Quebec the St. Lawrence has no value as a line of defence. it is on the contrary an element of weakness, because of its continguity to the American frontier, its interposition between centers of population and from the inherent weakness of rivers as lines of resistance.

Six or more canals have been constructed to circumvent rapids in the course of the river, all, excepting one above Montreal, to the north of it. They have all the vulnerability of works of this kind and add to the difficulties of defence. The Welland canal skirts the Niagara River circumventing the great fall between Ontario and Erie and it, therefore, connects the St. Lawrence with the great lakes. It is peculiarly exposed to attack throughout its length. The rapids of the St Mary's river, the outlet of Lake Superior, are avoided by a fine ship canal on the American side, which would require protection in the event of war if only as a precautionary measure of economy.*

---

*The following notes show the present status of navigation on the St. Lawrence and the Great Lakes:

In the sundry civil appropriation bill, the Fifty-third Congress, third session, 1895, provided that the President of the United States be authorized to appoint three persons who should have the power "to meet and confer with any similar committee which may be appointed by the Government of Great Britain or of the Dominion of Canada, and who shall make inquiry and report whether it is feasible to build such canals as shall enable vessels engaged in ocean commerce to pass to and fro between the Great Lakes and the Atlantic Ocean, with an adequate and controllable supply of water for continual use. where such canals can be most conveniently located, the probable cost of the same, with estimates in detail; and if any part of the same should be built in the territory of Canada, what regulations or treaty arrangements would be necessary between the United States and Great Britain to secure the free use of such canal to the people of this country at all times, with every necessary facts and considerations relating to the construction of the deep water channels between the Great Lakes and the Atlantic Ocean." Writing

Roads. The Canadian roads are very much like those in the United States excepting those in the neighborhood of large cities They connect all places of any considerable size but outside of them the country is impracticable for troops. Much bad weather or the passage of trains breaks them up, sometimes to the extent of being impassible, but the same is more or less true of all but the best European highways.*

Navy and shipping. While the bulk of the English navy is distant and might be embarrassed by complications elsewhere, its aid would be extended to Canada in time of war to the utmost extent possible. In point of shipping Canada stands, practically, on a par with the United States and she has from 70,000 to 80,000 sailors schooled in her great fisheries. With the active aid of the mother country this is so great an element of power that it has been proposed to abandon any preparation for land defence and to concentrate all expenditure in maintaining a force of cruisers to assist England in the event of war and, in case of war with

---

of this project from Ottawa, under date of June 11, 1895, a correspondent of the New York *Evening Post* says in part:

"The Dominion Government is about to appoint a departmental commission for the same purpose, and it is expected that the two bodies will meet, and, if possible, arrive at a common plan An international convention, held at Toronto last fall, recommended that the route should be deepened to 21 feet and a canal of the same depth constructed from the St. Lawrence to the Hudson, either by way of the Mohawk or by enlarging the existing channel of the Richelieu River and Champlain Canal, the whole work to be done at the joint expense of the United States and Canada and to be subject to their joint control."

"Canada has spent about $50,000,000 on the St. Lawrence route to secure a 14-foot channel. From the Strait of Belle Isle to Duluth is 2,385 statute miles, of which 72 are artificial and 2,313 open navigation. The artificial navigation can be deepened to 21 feet for about $30,000,000. The cost of enlarging the Richelieu and Champlain route to connect Montreal with Albany and New York City is not accurately known, nor has any estimate been formed of the cost of building a canal by the Mohawk Some engineers recommend that instead of going by the Mohawk or the Richelieu it would be better to build a canal from Montreal to Lake Champlain. The entire project is still in the nebulous form."

"The navigation of the Gulf of St. Lawrence was made free to both nations by the treaty of 1783, that of the River St. Lawrence by the Washington treaty of 1871. But the key to the navigation of the river lies in the Canadian canals between Montreal and Kingston, and between Lake Ontario and Lake Erie The Welland Canal, joining these two lakes, is 14 feet deep and the lower canals will soon be that depth; at present their greatest depth is 9 feet. The fleet of large steamers, 300 in number, plying west of Buffalo, is thus literally shut up in the upper lakes; in other words, the St. Lawrence route to tidewater is available only to the smaller lake craft, and till a depth of 21 feet is obtained from end to end the cost of transportation can not be materially reduced."

The New York *Journal of Commerce* of June 17, 1895, says in part: "On Thursday a ship canal at the falls of St. Marys River, the outlet of

---

*Compilers of text books are easy to find in accounts of the Franco-German campaigns, the writers, however, had probably no conception of the sometimes bottomless condition of

the United States, to give that nation ample employment in protecting her own commerce and sea coasts.

Frontiers. Measured on the railway, it is 3,700 miles from Halifax to Vancouver. If this be divided roughly into 3, the eastern third will contain the old and settled provinces of Nova Scotia, New Brunswick, Quebec and Ontario the western half of the middle third is the fertile, wheat producing province of Manitoba, the eastern half being the wilderness lying north and northwest of Lake Superior: the western third is divided in half by the Rocky mountains, east of which is a long stretch of barrens while west of them is the agricultural province of British Columbia. From the head of Lake Huron west to the ocean this frontier may be accepted as a straight line: eastward of that point are the three reentering angles, Sault St. Marie—Detroit—Kingston, Kingston—Lake Megantic—Riviere du Loup and Riviere du Loup—St. Andrew—Moncton

Railways. The conspicuous strategic feature of the Dominion is the Canadian Pacific Railroad There are numerous other

Lake Superior, was opened, and it affords to navigation much greater facilities than the canal on the American side which is now in use, but the American canal which will be opened next year will in its turn surpass the Canadian canal in general capacity, though the Canadian canal will remain superior in two dimensions These canals and their locks may be spoken of interchangeably, because in each case the canal consists simply in the lock and the channels approaching it. It is only fourteen years since the present American canal was opened, and yet the growth of the lake commerce was so rapid that the construction of a new lock was begun six years ago. The inadequacy of the lock now in use became apparent before it was opened for commerce, but when it was projected a lock 515 feet long and carrying 17 feet of water on the sills in a favorable stage of water seemed likely to respond to all demands upon it for many years to come.'

"The Canadian lock, which in rapidity of construction has outstripped ours. is 900 feet long, 60 feet wide and 22 feet deep Of our new lock, the masonry work is completed, and all the gates will be completed this summer, but nearly a year's work remains on the approaches. The lock is 800 feet long, 100 feet wide, and a steamer drawing 21 feet of water can pass through it Though shorter than the Canadian lock, its superficial area is 80,000 feet, and that of the Canadian canal 54,000 feet. The American canal lock will accommodate four of the largest lake steamers at the same time The depth of the lock is as great as there will be any occasion for until the lake ports generally are deepened. The two largest and finest passenger steamers on the lakes, the *Northwest*, which was put on the route last year, and the *North Land*, which has begun her career this year, and which compare not unfavorably with Atlantic passenger steamers, excepting a very few of the champion racers, draw, we believe, but 17 feet of water. It seems unlikely at present that steamers drawing more than 21 feet will ever be desired on the lakes.'

Observation and experience have proven that in the St. Lawrence canals themselves, at certain periods of low water, a depth of 9 feet can not be maintained. It should be noted that on account of the rapidity of the current, the rapids which they avoid are impossible to boats *ascending* the river, but mo t of them can be passed on the *downward* trip by strongly built vessels not too heavily laden.

Between Montreal and Rouse Po..iles, with a lock and dam at St Ours, on t.. C..b................the rapids of that name, admitting vessels of 6f feet at t lines with their branches but these lie gathered in a net work within two of the reentering angles of the frontier which have been mentioned. In speaking of the Pacific road it will be convenient to include as part of its system the Intercolonial road from Halifax to Quebec, skirting the Gulf of St. Lawrence and then the right bank of the river, and a second line of rails from St. John and St. Andrew to the St. Lawrence at Riviere du Loup, skirting the eastern and northern boundary of Maine * After clearing the great salient of Maine the system, on its way to the Atlantic, turns sharply to the south through New Brunswick seeking harbors which are open for a part of or all winter, and finds terminal points at Dalhousie, Chatham, Moncton, St. John, St. Andrew and, ultimately, at Halifax. All of these places are on good harbors and for most of these fortifications are proposed. Navigation in all of them excepting Halifax is subject to interruption by ice. Halifax is an extensive naval station and strongly fortified. A main terminal branch runs, almost directly, from St. John s N. B. to Montreal, through the entire breadth of the State of Maine, the course of the great system there as well as at other places hapily indicating that an invasion of Canada from the United States is purely a subjective theme. The road proper follows from Quebec to Montreal the left bank of the St. Lawrence and the Ottawa to the capital, where it crosses and runs to Sudbury, forming with the Ottawa river the base of the Detroit triangle. At Sudbury it throws out its last feeler, via the Sault St Mary to the United States, before it stretches out through the wilderness to find a new center of railroads and population, controlling the grain of Manitoba and the North West. at Winnipeg. Of Quebec it may be said that it is a fortress and that, however incomplete, it is, conventionally speaking, impregnable On the right bank of the river are modern works which command a railroad center and which "occupy the ground from which Wolfe shelled the town." "Frost prevents the possibility of a winter investment by a modern army and limits the time of any investment to five summer months; and even in summer the mighty sweep of the St. Lawrence renders complete investment almost an impossibility to an invader." Winnipeg, at the other end of this section is only about 50 miles from the United States line at Pembina and could be easily occupied and held. Some 100 miles from the Pacific, the road crosses the Fraser river and runs on the right bank to its western terminus at Vancouver-New

---

*It is ... at the construction both of the Pacific and of the Intercolonial roads was su ... by strategical considerations,—that of the former by the Sepoy rebellion and of ... a crisis of complications with the United States

Westminister For one-half of this distance it is within 25 miles of the boundary. Vancouver has a good harbor, easily accessible by the Straits of Georgia, both banks of which are commanded by English batteries. Vancouver itself, is easily defensible. A great naval station is projected either there or at Victoria and Esquimault on Vancouver Island, but it must be evident that here as at the Atlantic terminus all efforts aim at preserving the integrity of a great navy, that wherever its fleets may be in a wide world of waters they may be at home.

All Canadian railways are single track, have the standard American guage and are well managed, with American routine. As far as the long, single lines which run parallel to the frontier are concerned they are not a rapid, safe or certain means of transporting troops while the American railroads offer no important parallel the destruction of which would affect concentration. The Canadian lines in the Detroit triangle are continuations of American systems and against them the resources of the west could be concentrated at Detroit and those from the east at Buffalo. The throat of the eastern net-work of roads is at St. John (Quebec) which lies about half way between Rouse Point and Montreal and two days short marches from either place. It commands, also, the Richelieu River canal.

England has three great routes to the east: Liverpool—Canada—Yokohoma, 12,000; Southampton—Suez—Calcutta, 8600 miles, Liverpool—Cape Town—Calcutta, 13,000; (Yokohoma—Shanghai—Hong-Kong—Singapore—Calcutta, 5600 miles, completes the circuit). For the British Empire, uninterrupted communication between the mother country and her possessions beyond the seas is a question, almost, of life and death.

In mileage, the route via Canada to Japan is not very much shorter than the route via Suez, but the Canadian rails not only economize time but avoid whatever of peril the navigation of the Straits of Malacca and the China seas involves As a route to some of her East-Asiatic stations the Canadian Pacific may or may not be favorable, according to circumstances, but in any case it cannot be an advantageous route to India or to the south eastern Asiatic ports, for the distances via Suez or via Cape Town are so much shorter that the Canadian rails cannot compete in economizing time. The latter would therefore seem to be of strategic importance to British interests, only in the Northern Pacific ocean.

To assure its integrity in time of war the Suez canal route calls for extraordinary expenditure in time of peace, and for tireless vigilance. Gibraltar, Malta, Cyprus, Egypt and a great fleet on its waters, may make of the Mediteranean, for the time being, an Anglo-Saxon sea; but the Latin races will claim that it belongs more naturally to them, while France with a strong navy, with her Mediteranean ports and with Tunis, will decline, for long, to allow communication with her Asiatic possessions through the canal, to be endangered. Finally it is claimed that the Suez canal may be easily rendered useless by means of high explosives.

Under these circumstances it is not surprising to find much of the best professional opinion in England in favor of ending the costly occupancy of the Mediteranean, together with the irritation of which it is a perennial source. It is pointed out that the route via the Cape of Good Hope is without disadvantages other than its length and that with the command of the sea and with Sierra Leone, Ascension, St. Helena, Mauritius and Ceylon, England may consider this route peculiarly her own.

The foregoing examples are intended to illustrate widely differing conditions. In the case of two military powers the choice of a theatre of operations will be generally limited from causes which are constant, and are thoroughly well understood; and success will depend mainly on preparation and training. An opposite extreme is a case like that of Texas, where it is desirable to occupy abruptly a country about which comparatively little is known, where the conditions which exist, some of them only for the time being, must be ascertained promptly and, at the same time, very accurately, and where the soundest judgment will be called for· because these conditions and their bearing, while new and unfamiliar to any one who is without experience in war, offer in their combinations a wide field for choice to a skillful and prudent leader.

In fixing, from time to time, the boundary line between Canada and the United States, the possibility of war between the two countries must have seemed very remote. It runs between two industrial communities, and these have worked to facilitate rather than restrict natural intercourse. Were both of equal extent, population and wealth it might be hard to decide which would be placed at a disadvantage in time of war, by the conformation of the frontier. In no sense is any part of this a military frontier, and the presence of a fortress like Quebec, however material, is purely incidental: while on both sides the quantity of war ma terial and the number of troops immediately available is insignificant when compared to the extent of front. In a case like this, conditions which have not been created but are none the less hard and fast, will limit the choice of a theatre as a fortress and camp and hostile armies can not do. They may be summarized in that lack of preparation which will demand the use of whatever means there are to strike whatever blow is possible, at a time and from a direction which will be fixed by stubborn and inelastic terms.

With the aid of good maps it would be instructive to select theatres of operation and to devise plans of campaign if the student could submit them afterwards to tests which involve a great deal of skill and work, and, finally, to the crucial review of experienced leaders. A plan of campaign may be stated very briefly and in a few sentences, but it should be ventilated by means of remorseless figures, rather than by discussion in an essay, however interesting. Books and writing are valuable just so far as they do not interfere with practical duties. These, *if wisely ordered*, will best develop, from day to day, the soldierly qualities with which an officer is endowed.

IV.

THEATRE OF OPERATIONS. OCCUPATION. *Transport by Water.*
In treating of the military geography of Canada, the aid which could or would be extended to the Dominion by England was not discussed, because there is some difference of opinion concerning the feasibility of transferring an army to a theatre of war beyond the sea.

With proper facilities transportation by water has many advantages. Schemes for embarking and debarking must be well thought out in advance and plans must be adopted, for the rapid alteration of the interior arrangements of merchant vessels which are known to be available; otherwise their accomodating power will vary greatly and will be in some cases too limited to be of service.

The Great Powers possess very few troop-ships and these are kept up only for the regular service of reliefs.[*] In case of war they would, of course, be available at once, but for the transport of large bodies of troops reliance is placed on the merchant marine.

Water transport avoids the hardships of marching, is seven or eight times faster and as far as the subsequent condition of the troops is concerned, compares favorably with long journeys by rail.

River transport.—Where navigable rivers and water ways are available their use is exceedingly convenient and advantageous. In the United States the water ways and especially the western rivers are peculiarly adapted for it and western steamboats are almost ideal as means of transportation. During the War of Secession large numbers of these were moored, overlapping each other, their bows run into the banks almost wherever they might select: troops and animals were marched onto the boats assigned them, with no delay to speak of, while the large deck space below, open at the sides offered ample room, while the open boiler arrangements offered facilities for cooking. Stores and forage were quickly rolled on board, the work being facilitated at night by fires on the bank. The fleet would then move in single file, preceded and followed by gunboats and, if large, with gunboats at intervals in the column. It was sometimes necessary to land and drive away artillery or sharpshooters who menaced it

---
[*]According to the Gotha Calender, 1895, Great Britain has nine

from shore, and pilot houses were provided with bullet proof shields Light, specially selected troops, were held ready to land from boats provided with wide gang planks. In case of necessity these boats ran promptly in shore, the gang plank was lowered with special tackle and the troops landed and deployed on the run. The advance boat usually carried the Commandant of the expedition and he signaled his orders by means of a preconcerted code of steam whistle blasts, a copy of which was posted on every boat. By combinations of long and short whistles, repeated from boat to boat, these signals covered numerous contingencies, e. g., "look out for right (or left) bank," "let me go ahead and reconnoiter,' "tie up for the night on right bank," "close up," "boat No. —— take the lead, to land troops," &c

These steamboats averaged 500 tons and one of them could carry supplies for an army corps for 3 or 4 days. Compared with a railway train, one boat was considered equal to 40 or 50 cars, or about two trains. The long river trips were a veritable period of rest for the overmarched Federal troops. Officers and men returning from a campaign in the interior, would receive their pay and back mails, again have access to their baggage and enjoy regular sleep and comfortable meals.

In the autumn of 1864, General A. J. Smith's corps, about 17,000 men, 3500 animals and 450 vehicles, was sent from Memphis to St. Louis on steamboats. After driving General Price's forces out of Missouri, marching through that State into Kansas and return, it reembarked at St. Louis, was transported to Nashville, Tenn., took part in the great battle and, in pursuit of Hood's army, reached the Tennessee River at Eastport, Miss. Met here again by transports, it was sent down the Tennessee, Ohio and Mississippi Rivers to New Orleans and thence by water to Mobile Bay, taking part there in the storming of the defences and the capture of the city. In about six months, with about 40 steamboats, the corps traveled some 4000 miles, reinforced three armies and engaged in three campaigns.

"Rivers, when of sufficient volume, form the most appropriate of all channels of communication with the interior of continents. The greater or lesser degree of uniformity in the volumn of water in a river along its course depends on the manner in which its supply is obtained. In certain zones, the supply comes from the rains which fall on the uplands, and a certain uniformity is thus maintained through the greater part of the year, in others it depends mainly on the melting of the snows, and rivers so fed are only fed during the summer months The rivers which have their origin in the Alps, for example, attain their highest level in the month of June, and their lowest in January. Rivers, on the other hand, which are not fed by the melting of the snows, have their highest level from January to April, and the lowest from July to October. The Congo receives its waters from north and south of the equator where the rain falls at different periods of the year; consequently, it is always full. In some regions evaporation nearly equals the amount of the rainfall, and the depth of rivers there is never great, in others the water is absorbed by the sands and is lost before it reaches the sea'"

During Banks' Red River Expedition in the War of Secession a portion of Admiral Porter's Mississippi Squadron had ascended the river, keeping pace with the troops operating on shore, and when these were checked and were obliged to fall back, found itself above the rapids at Alexandria. The river was falling rapidly and if the troops continued to retreat the gunboats would be captured, provided they could not pass the rapids which would then in all probability be impossible. Believing that their capture or destruction would involve the blockade of the Mississippi and perhaps greater disaster, Lieutenant-Colonel Joseph Baily, 4th Wisconsin cavalry, on April 9th, proposed to Major-General Franklin to increase the depth of water by means of a dam and submitted to him his plans for the same. General Franklin favored and urged the scheme but owing to want of confidence in its feasibility on the part of higher commanders and to other delays the necessary orders for working parties, tools, teams, &c., were not obtained until the 30th.

The width of the river at the point where the dam was built (the foot of the rapids) was 758 feet and the depth, 4 to 6 feet. The current was very rapid, running about 10 miles per hour. Two wing dams were also constructed at the head of the falls. The increase in depth by the main dam was 5 feet 4½ inches; by the wing dams 1 foot 2 inches, total 6 feet 6½ inches. On its completion, May 8th, the entire fleet passed over the rapids to a place of safety below.

Commander Mahan, U. S. Navy, writes,* in part, of this remarkable work as follows· "Twelve feet were thought necessary before going up, a depth usually found from March to June. At the very least seven were needed by the gunboats to go down, and on the 30th of April there were actually 3 feet 4 inches. Ten gunboats and two tugs were thus imprisoned in a country soon to

---

*"The Navy in the Civil War."

pass into the enemy's hands by the retreat of the army." * *
* "But Bailey had the faith that moves mountains, and he was
moreover happy in finding at his hands the fittest tools for the
work Among the troops in the far southwest were two or three
regiments from Maine, the northeasternmost of all the States
These had been woodmen and lumbermen from their youth,
among their native forests, and a regiment of them now turned
trained and willing arms upon the great trees on the north shore
of the Red River, and there were many others who, on a smaller
scale and in different scenes, had experience in the kind of work
now to be done Time was pressing and from two to three thous-
and men were at once set to work. The falls are about a mile
in length, filled with rugged rocks which, at this low water, were
bare or nearly so, the water rushing down around, or over, them
with great swiftness. From the north bank was built what was
called the "tree dam," formed of large trees laid with the current, the branches interlocking, the trunks down stream and
cross-tied with heavy timber, upon this was thrown brush, brick,
and stone, and the weight of water as it rose bound the fabric
more closely down upon the bottom of the river From the
other bank, where the bottom was more stony and trees less
plenty, great cribs were pushed out, sunk and filled with stone
and brick—the stone brought down the river in flat-boats, the
bricks obtained by pulling down deserted brick buildings. On
this side, a mile away, was a large sugar-house, this was torn
down and the whole building, machinery, and kettles went to ballast the dam. Between the cribs and the tree-dam a length of
150 feet was filled by four large coal barges, loaded with brick
and sunk. This great work was completed in eight working
days." * * *

"The dam was finished, the water rising, and three boats below, when on the 9th the pressure became so great as to sweep
away two of the barges in midstream and the pent-up water
poured through." The gap was only 66 feet wide and through
this opening four more vessels steered, taking all the chances and
reaching the safe water below with some little damage. "The
work on the dam had been done almost wholly by the soldiers,
who had worked both day and night, often up to their waists and
even to their necks in the water, showing throughout the utmost
cheerfulness and good humor. The partial success that followed
the first disappointment of the break, was enough to make such
men go to work again with good will Bailey decided not to try
again, with his limited time and materials, to sustain the whole

weight of water with one dam; and so, leaving the gap untouched, went on to build two wing-dams on the upper falls. These, extending from from either shore towards the middle of the river and inclining slightly down stream, took part of the weight, causing a rise of 1 foot 2 inches, and shed the water from either side into the channel between them. Three days were needed to build these, one a crib and the other a tree-dam, and a bracket dam a little lower down to help guide the current "

Transport by sea. Tonnage.—The exact meaning of the term tonnage as applied to vessels requires explanation because it expresses sometimes weight and sometimes carrying capacity. A war-ship is designed to meet certain service conditions or, in other words, to carry a maximum weight, which is fairly constant, without exceeding a certain maximum draught of water Her tonnage is expressed by the weight of water in tons, which is displaced when she is immersed to the load-line, and this applies to all war-ships and possibly to a few others, mainly government vessels.

Displacement tonnage is not applicable to merchant ships because it is necessary to ascertain the space available for storing a remunerative cargo, and the draught to which they can be safely laden varies with the nature of the cargo, the length of the voyage and even with the season of the year. Their tonnage is measured and registered that they may be equitably assessed for port dues and charges; is ascertained by a system of rules adopted by law known as the Moorsom (British) system, adopted essentially, by all maritime nations, and which embraces certain concessions to ship owners which make it advantageous "to build strong, fast-sailing and good sea-going ships, with ample accommodations for the crew. Tonnage denoting carrying capacity is called "register tonnage," and the rules for finding it are very full and elaborate. The measurements which they impose result in formulae which are applicable in finding displacement tonnage also, both designations being based on cubic content

Displacement tonnage may be found approximately by calculating the cubic content of a parallelopipedon whose volume equals the product of the length on load-line with the breadth and mean draught, and taking 45% of this for fast cruisers, 55% for vessels of common form and 60% for battleships, and assuming one cubic foot of sea water to weigh 64 pounds, Designating the tonnage of war vessels by their displacement can hardly be satisfactory excepting in so far as increased displacement indicates increased fighting power. Dues are not assessed on displacement tonnage, and in the case of war vessels passing through the Suez canal the dues are assessed on a tonnage based on an assumed carrying capacity

Registered tonnage Gross register tonnage expresses, in tons of 100 cubic feet, the total capacity of the hold and deck-houses of a vessel. Net register tonnage is obtained by deducting from the gross all spaces not available for remunerative service, is that on which dues are paid and is usually called, simply, register tonnage. As has been stated, the rules for finding the gross tonnage are very elaborate but it may be found approximately by taking the product of inside measurements of upper-deck length, main breadth and midship depth, dividing by 100 and multiplying by .6 to 8, according as the vessel approaches the "full-form" or "clipper." To find the net tonnage deduct from the gross tonnage the compartments actually occupied by, or actually appropriated to the use of, the crew, including officers, but not to exceed 5% of the gross tonnage; also the space actually occupied by, or required to be enclosed for the proper working of, the boilers and machinery, plus 50% of such space for paddle-wheels and 75% for screw-shaft· but the total deduction for these spaces shall not exceed 50% of the gross tonnage. As this limitation tends to give crew and boiler-room their full allowance of space the net tonnage of a steamer will be, as a rule, about 50% of her gross tonnage From 5% to 10% should be deducted from this to allow for space which cannot be made accessible for men, animals or stores, when the net tonnage available for troops may be safely taken at from 40% to 45% of the gross.

There is, of course, no relation between tons space and tons weight, but an arbitrary one has been adopted based on the average weight of mixed cargoes. Freight is charged per ton of 40 cubic feet, if 2000 pounds or less; exceeding 2000 pounds it is charged at total dead weight. The dead weight which a vessel can carry depends on her "reserve of buoyancy," which is the volumn and buoyancy of the part of a ship not immersed but which may be made water-tight. The number of tons weight which a ship can carry will always greatly exceed the number which expresses her register tonnage. The "load-line" marks the limit of immersion. It is located by law in Great Britain but not in the United States.

Transport by sea.—This subject has received some attention in England but not as much as it deserves A nation which has possessions in all parts of the world, together with the uncontested command of the sea, a large merchant marine, and a very respectable number of fine troops at home, should find it interesting and important. As late as January, 1894, however, there seems to have existed some diversity of opinion, even there, concerning it. In a lecture and discussion before the Military Society of Ireland at that time, the lecturer, Captain James, said· "There is a very mistaken notion about the amount of shipping which is required for the transportation of troops. Troops can be packed like herrings in a barrel for a short voyage. For instance, when the French went to the Crimea they took, I believe, some 2000 men in one line of battleship, and if it were possible to do this in those days, it is certainly possible to do much more in these days with the hugh steamers which now exist. As a practical fact, there was a great discussion some years ago at the United Service Institution, London, and it was shown by Lord Wolseley that there was always present in French ports a sufficient amount of ships to transport 100,000 men without any difficulty whatever." * * * "We could certainly command the whole French coast with a proper fleet, and, if so, we could throw our troops—the 100,000 men I spoke of—anywhere along the coast of Europe, from the Baltic to the Black Sea, without any great difficulty " (From England to the Black Sea is over 3000 miles by water) Captain Copley said that he did "not know where we would get ships first of all to move 100,000 men at one time, and secondly, I think it extremely doubtful even if you can get the shipping and the men, that they could be moved without the enemy becoming aware of it;" indicating thereby that a descent on the coast must be a surprise to succeed. General, Lord Wolseley, in closing the discussion, said: "Now, as the conveyance by sea of an army—say, three army corps and a strong cavalry division, 100,000 men—which the lecturer said could be easily moved by us from one part of the world to the other—I worked out this question many years ago, and as well as I remember, to convey such an army from England to France it would take 150 large-sized steamers and no more. For a voyage, say to Constantinople, which is about the farthest point to which we are ever likely to send that number of men and speaking roughly from memory, I believe that 300 large-sized steamers would suffice, and 300 ships could be easily collected in England at any time." * * * "The lecturer proposed, not only that we should be always able to protect England against invasion, but have the power of striking an offensive blow beyond the seas, with an army of 100,000 men complete in every requirement. If we had during war a regular army, in England, between the militia and volunteers, 150,000 men, we should always be in a position to carry out the lecturer's proposal. It may be taken as an actual certainty, that we should never send abroad an army were it in any way possible for an enemy to invade us There can be no doubt that the despatch of a force abroad, would be of enormous benefit to England in bringing to a rapid conclusion any war she became involved in If in any such war we had at home a thoroughly equipped force of the proposed strength ready to be embarked for active service, that fact would give us an enormous power, and consequently a very great influence in the world, and no nation would lightly go to war with us."

Difficulties inherent in this method of transport are; the necessity for convoy should the enemy possess war vessels, difficulties of ventilation, lighting and cooking and providing proper and sufficient exercise for the men; the construction, maintenance and inspection of closet and washing arrangements; the storage of arms, accoutrements, baggage, &c. in convenient, safe and accessible places, police arrangements, consideration of cleanliness and prevention of contagious diseases All these things are inevitably complicated by sea-sickness. a few hours of rough weather with closed hatches, puts the between-decks, when occupied by troops, in a horrible condition. No matter how favorable circumstances of weather may be when embarking troops for even a short voyage by sea, it is well to take the same precautions as if sailing into the teeth of a storm for an indefinite period. In March, 1873, the Artillery School battalion embarked at Fort Monroe for Washington, a 12 hours trip in a land-locked bay The weather at starting was warm and pleasant but before midnight the vessel was battling against a dangerous storm with ice-encrusted decks, which made it necessary to crowd the command into the limited cabin space.

Transport by sea is difficult in proportion to the length of the voyage; and the varying capacity and internal arrangements of vessels make it impracticable to adopt other than very flexible rules by which to estimate the size of armies that can be transported. In military matters, however, it is folly to say what can or can not be done, given favorable conditions and an intrepid and enterprising genius in command.

The command of the sea.—An indispensible condition is the full or at least ample command of the sea, even if only for the time being in a particular region. This has been recently illustrated by the sinking of a Chinese transport by a Japanese cruiser "and in the narrow escape of the Chinese reinforcements for their army in the Korea." As long ago as 1871, Captain Hoseason, R. N , contended that by virtue of having command of the sea, England was no longer merely a great naval nation, but a great military nation also,—the first military nation in the world He bases his conclusions on the argument that England, with the command of the sea, if she will keep on hand a sufficient number of transport ships in addition to available merchant steamers will, in case of war, have the widest possible selection of bases of operation, any one of which she can occupy in the most efficient and economical manner, by steam water-transport: thus avoiding the necessity for keeping a large force over the entire line of communications with a great sacrifice of men, animals and material as in case of a base of operations on land. He claims that, "the transport of horses, and of all kinds of munitions of war, including the heaviest ordnance, is an operation of no difficulty in the present day, and the rapidity and economy of such mode of transport is perfectly marvelous " "It is by an efficient steam fleet conveying a flying army, that we shall possess the power to keep the coast line of an enemy in a fever of alarm; no town within 15 or 20 miles of the sea should be safe from a nocturnal visit, and the terror which a well-organized flying army acting on an enemy's coast would create, must paralyze a force of twenty times its strength." "The commercial interests of this country are so widely spread, that it is impossible to forsee the moment when our forces will again be called into the field, or with what nation we may be next engaged; but one fact is most apparent, that our chief power lies in the rapidity and economy of our transport by sea, which our wealth and our command of the ocean enable us fully to develope." "Our success in ocean steam navigation has long justified us in disregarding distance, and enabled us to resolve all questions upon war to the one element— time The economy of steam transport over every kind of land transport is so great that we may be assured of the power of exhausting the strength of any nation with whom we may be at war, without seeking to engage them in any vast numbers, it is disease and exposure which tell upon an army harrassed by long marches and counter-marches The deaths in the field of battle are as nothing to the loss thus inflicted, and more especially if the enemy should have an extended coast-line, and efficient steam sea-base therefore, is of vital importance to secure success to our military operations, and it is certain that any amount of land transport can be conveyed by sea most rapidly and economically, for the world's resources are open to that nation which holds the dominion of the seas." "It will be perceived at a glance, how impossible it would be to defend Canada, in the event of any hostilities with America, by any amount of British troops which we might retain in that country; but most important aid could be rendered by a counter-attack, made by a combined naval and military force along the entire coast-line of America, and having for its base of operations so many important colonial possessions." Fast ocean liners carrying troops will not, it is claimed, require convoy, because they can outsail the fastest cruisers

Number of vessels required.—A simple rough rule is to allow 2½ tons per man, 7 tons per animal for the longest voyages This is ample and includes every allowance for arms, ammunition, wagons and vehicles of every description, rations, forage and stores. The stores comprise camp and garrison equipage, clothing, tools, &c , and the provisions full rations for 6 weeks and forage for the same time The space demanded for the fodder for the horses is comparatively very small, while water in ample quantities can be condensed daily from sea water. Rations in original packages, properly stowed, correspend in dead weight to ordinary mixed cargoes, and an ordinary coasting steamer can carry provisions for 50,000 men for a month Vehicles would, of course, be taken apart and packed in the smallest space possible.

This rough allowance will hold good with large steamers of about 4000 tons gross register each, and Lord Wolseley must have had ships of this capacity in view when he spoke of transporting 100,000 men in 300 large-sized steamers. The carrying capacity for troops, of smaller vessels, decreases disproportionately with their size.

The embarkation would take place at several ports simultaneously, where the demands of commerce have provided commodious docks and wharfs, steam-cranes, electric lighting, &c : modern appliances offer also increased facilities for debarkation, e. g , specially constructed steam or electric launches for towing floats, and notably, flat bottomed, light draft vessels.

The collection, purchase or chartering, alteration and adaptation of merchant vessels for transports is sure to be slow It is probable that no nation has sufficient tonnage lying idle, as it were, for 40,000 troops, or to begin embarking them until the sixth day after the order reaches the ships. The collection of the ships necessary to transport an additional 60,000 men would be subject to many delays, even in England· but with her enormous tonnage there is no reason for supposing that the withdrawal of

300 of her large steamers from commerce would endanger her food supply, as has been freely stated.

To land French troops in Italy, a voyage of from 3 to 5 days, 3 tons are allowed for an animal and ⅔ tons for a man. With an allowance of ½ ton per man troops are much crowded, but it has often been deemed sufficient for trips of 36 hours. In all cases there is a tendency to put more men on ships than is compatible with their comfort and health, and this must be vigilantly guarded against by the highest authortty, for, at the last moment, a subordinate commander cannot well refuse to embark his men, no matter how inadequate the accommodations are that are furnished him. Naturally the most available vessels are those which, for the time being, are unemployed, and these will always include all those that for one reason or another are undesirable, frequently unseaworthy. This kind comes to the front promptly when the government is seeking vessels at remunerative rates.

The British expedition to Egypt in 1882, as far as the transportation of troops is concerned was very successful. "Between July 30th and August 12th, 41 large transports were despatched to the seat of war; advantage was taken of numerous excellent ports, so that the despatch of troops and stores was going on from several ports at the same moment, and yet without the least interference one with another. 13 sailed from London, 11 from Southampton, 9 from Portsmouth, 2 from Liverpool, 3 from Kingston, one from Queenstown and one from Woolwich." "Each unit embarked on board its own ship, with its transport and tentage complete. To each infantry battalion was allotted one ship, each of which carried, on an average, about 30 officers and 760 men, with 55 horses, 2 water carts, 10 two-wheeled carts, and about 150 tents of sorts. The cavalry had two ships per regiment, each of which carried, on an average, 13 officers, 290 men, and 270 horses, with water-cart and 3 two-wheeled carts, while a proportion of small-arm ammunition carts and forage wagons were taken. The artillery had one ship per battery, averaging 7 officers, 170 men, and 130 to 180 horses, and, of course, their guns, ammunition, and stores. The ammunition column had one ship, carrying 185 officers and men, and 207 horses, with the ammunition reserve. The engineers were similarly provided for in separate ships, as also were the base hospitals and other departments." In all, about 70 large steamers (including storeships) were required for about 24,000 men.

Descents on hostile coasts.—The history of war is replete with accounts of descents or attempted descents on hostile coasts. In almost every case success or want of success can be traced directly to the personal character and qualifications of the leader. *In modern times steam power has placed immense power at command of expeditionary forces "in the way of certainty of transportation to their destination by any fixed date, and the speed with which the seas can be traversed. No longer at the mercy of winds and currents, an expeditionary force is now a mobile instrument in the hands of its commander, capable of being placed at will exactly where required, and rapidly transferred from one point to another Moreover, there is now the certainty of co-operation, if so required, between forces starting from points far apart, and the power of threatening one point of a hostile coast, and then effecting the actual descent upon some quite different spot." "Probably in all countries the communications around the coast-line are very indifferent, and the transfer of troops from one point to another along the coast by land is a slow and difficult operation. But, on the other hand, an expeditionary force, packed in swift steamers, is capable of being shifted in a few hours from any point to some other widely separated from it. The land forces of the defenders, once set in motion towards any given point of the coast, cannot readily be afterwards diverted."**

Descents have been successfully made in opposition to naval preponderance. In 1796 the French descended on Ireland, in 44 vessels, 8 days out, penetrating without loss a triple line of English ships; and Napoleon evaded the English fleet on the expedition to Egypt.

Whether an isolated country, like the United States, with a long coast line and many bays, inlets and harbors, can be invaded by any considerable European force, is a question concerning which differences of opinion are known to exist A coalition of European powers against her would be very formidable, and considering the Monroe Doctrine, exclusive tariffs, the asylum offered to political offenders, the Nicaragua Canal, American indifference to foreign opinion, &c , such a coalition seems at least possible † When there is a great extent of favorable beach, there seems to be nothing to prevent the invader steering for it and, favored by weather, landing without opposition. The guarding of a coast at every point requires a more extensive system of lookouts, signals, and coast guards than it is easy to furnish, or, at any rate, than exists. An army landing in this way must put itself sooner or later where it can get provisions, place its transports in safety and maintain communication with home, and this

---
*Major Elmslie, R A. the italics not in the original
†Written in 1893.

necessitates the occupation of a seaport. The capture and occupation of a seaport and harbor ab initio is not possible if it be defended by modern works. it can be made very difficult or greatly delayed by improvised defence.

Smooth water, i. e. favorable weather, is absolutely necessary for landing on a beach and the interruption of landing by a prolonged storm may mean failure or disaster: but climatic and weather conditions have long been a matter of special study; the results of which will be factors in any scheme, as to the time and place selected.

Light draught vessels, gun-boats and merchant steamers of 1500 tons displacement are now constructed drawing no more water than the ordinary harbor tug-boats. There are flat-bottom boats available with a carrying capacity of several hundred tons which have a draught of water under 2 feet and a speed of 15 miles an hour. These could simply be beached at low water, with a certainty of being floated with the tide and land troops in the most convenient fashion.

"An expeditionary force is now under full command. The modern, well-found steamers can keep together without the slightest difficulty, if required to do so. They will thus be easy to convoy, can make the land at any given point and hour desired, and after making an apparent descent upon one portion of the coast sufficient to attract the attention and troops of the defenders, can with great rapidity transfer the blow to some other and quite different spot, where the real debarkation can be effected." "The enemy's coast will be given as wide a berth as possible, a detour being made if necessary to keep the fleet outside the radius of torpedo-boat action, and the descent upon the coast, if attack by torpedo boats be a possibility, should be effected at right angles to the general coast-line, so that as short a time as possible is spent within the radius of their action."

A European coalition could dispose of several hundred swift torpedo-boats (England alone has over 200), and these could not only reconnoiter the coast but could enter all but the best protected harbors and destroy property· while the battleships and cruisers covered the transports and landing.

Descent on a hostile coast is the only military operation in which surprise on a large scale is any longer possible.

General Scott disembarked nearly 12,000 men at Vera Cruz, and landed Worth's division of 4500 men in 65 lighters of 100 men each by 4 o'clock P. M. These advanced simultaneously until they grounded, tne men landing waist deep, the lighters returning by 10 o'clock the remaining troops were on shore. Many if not all the horses were lowered or driven overboard and swam. The landing of equipage and supplies consumed several days. There was no confusion, accident or disaster and—it is fair to add—no opposition.

Embarking, &c.—Detailed instructions exist in all services for embarking and disembarking troops. Those for the U. S. service* are simple and clear and should be implicitly followed. The leader of an expeditionary force can have no more material concern than that of obtaining his own personal assurance that adequate, safe and comfortable transportation is furnished for his men and animals.

"When boats are under charter, it becomes most necessary for the quartermaster in charge to be exceedingly vigilant, or he will not get worth for the public money. Captains and crews under these circumstances appear to join hands to do as little work as possible." "The embarkation of troops should be carefully studied and provided for. The capacity of a ship should be ascertained and berths fitted up," including pegs &c for accoutrements, "cooking arrangements provided, abundance of water and ample stores secured for the whole voyage, with adequate surplus for emergencies All freight, stores and material should first go on board, and be stored so that what is needed on the voyage, is placed where it may be had promptly. If animals are to go with a command, they are loaded after the stores, and just before the men. After every other provision is made the men should go on board, and not until then.† The English regulations provide that a trooper shall embark with his horse.

"During the actual embarkation visitors should be excluded from the ships and wharves This enactment should be widely notified and rigidly enforced."

Proper ventilation of the space occupied by troops is not only necessary but is indispensable. Regulations for this may well be left to the medical staff, but they must be revised and enforced by the commander-in-chief.

It is very important that latrines should be large, easily accessible and well lighted and ventilated If possible, they should be on deck with a clear drop to the water.

---
*Manual of Heavy Artillery Service, 4th edition, page 325, et seq
†Major Lee U. S. Q M Department, in Journal of the Military Service Institution March, 1894. The same article contains practical rules f... care at sea of horses and mules, derived from the writer's experi... the Wa if necess... w en he had charge of the depot of Alexan ria, with 4... sea at... in 1000 to 3000 tons of coal per day, and from whence he shipped in one year... a... with exceedingly small loss.

The British regulations require that each ship should be able to distil daily one-fourth more than the regulation quantity of water for all on board. An allowance of one gallon per man and 7 or 8 gallons per animal per day is ample for all purposes. Water can be kept in iron and wooden tanks and in barrels. Large iron tanks measuring 4 feet in every direction are usually arranged in rows in the hold, resting on the ballast, water being drawn from these as required by means of a suction pump

After the stores are shipped and stowed the embarkation of men and animals is very rapid. *The vessel should then lie for about 24 hours in smooth water*, until everyone and everything is shaken down in place, so to speak, and so that order may arise out of what seems hopeless confusion before meeting rough water outside.

V.

Occupation of the Theatre of Operations Overland.—The process of transferring an army from a peace footing to a war footing is called mobilization The assemblement of the mobilized forces near the frontier of the state to be attacked is called concentration.

Mobilization "is the passage of all the units to the war footing. It is absolutely distinct from concentration. This principle appears trite to-day yet" in 1870 "the two operations were confounded" by the French, "and reciprocally embarrased one another."

"Formerly, at the commencement of the century, for example, a political rupture was visible a long time in advance, especially by the power that, counting upon a superiority of military resources, had resolved to take the offensive. It then prepared its forces in secret, assembled them with equal concealment, declared war when it was ready, and endeavored to bring on hostilities at once. To-day, with the development of intercourse, increase in the number of railroad and telegraph lines, and expansion of the influence of the press, such methods are no longer practicable. All preparations for war in view of an early offensive will immediately become known. Indeed, the character of the masses to be moved, no longer permits action under the same conditions. But if the assemblement of men and horses, in view of hostilities, can no longer be concealed, it can, on the other hand, be executed at the decisive moment with a promptness formerly unknown, and in a shorter space by one belligerent than by the other This is dependent upon the kind and degree of preparation in time of peace.'

"With the introduction of compulsory service, the opening of war has become a more critical moment than formerly, for the nations concerned It is no longer a question of sending against the enemy a portion of the young men organized as an active force, but the entire able-bodied population of a country is called out. From one to two millions of men must be rudly torn from the peaceful pursuits of ordinary life To them must be added from one to two hundred thousand horses. It is necessary to feed, group, equip and transport these masses with all the material required by them. This is a supreme ordeal which profoundly stirs the nation, reaches all households, all occupations."

"Now it is nothing to raise a regiment to the war effective. Difficult, however, is the execution of that great body of measures requiring simultaneous execution . the installation of new authorities ; the formation of new agencies , the organization of depots, interior garrisons, commands, special governments and station services ; the creation of new staffs from heterogeneous elements ; the organization of trains, parks, convoys, and accessory field services ; the assembling of horses, provisions, munitions, means of transport, &c. A simple enumeration of the details of such an operation makes it apparent how greatly confusion is to be feared, and how indispensable it is that minute preparations be made in time of peace."

"Still further reasons demand this. The mobolization must be effected as rapidly as possible, for the sooner it is finished, the sooner will the concentration be accomplished, provided the railroads lend themselves to a prompt transportation of troops. An army which concentrates upon a frontier more speedily than the enemy, possesses advantages which exercise a favorable influence upon the entire course of the campaign ' *

The term "mobilization" is applied improperly but conveniently to whatever preparation a nation may make to place armed forces in the field, however meagre the available war resources may be. The burden of improvising means of defense will fall on officers of the permanent establishment, and it will help them if they are familiar with the methods employed by military powers when placing their troops on a war footing. In all military powers these methods are now substantially the same and those of Germany may be taken as a model.

Mobilization of the German army. Each unit mobilises every year some portion of its personel or material. A field battery, for instance will furnish its guns complete on a war footing, another the wagons, another the horses, etc. The complete battery is exercised, marched, worked by train and brigaded for maneuver with an infantry command. The next year each of the batteries will mobilize a different portion and by this means all gain experience.

In actual mobilization the first and simplest operation is calling in the reserves and thereby, roughly speaking, doubling the

---
* Derrécagaix, modern war Foster's translation

strength of the establishment. This is simple because in Germany localization has been carried to its extreme limit, and each unit has its special recruiting ground. The country is divided into 17 corps districts, each of which is subdivided into 2 divisions and 4 brigade districts,—these, again, into regimental, battalion and company districts. The system of recruitment is so localized that every company comes from a certain village or group of small villages. Every town, village, hamlet, &c., has well protected sign-boards placed where the main roads enter it, setting forth the company, battalion, regiment, brigade, division and corps to which its men either belong or owe duty, together with much other information, chiefly the exact location of their equipment and stores. The unit is a regimental district, called the "Landwehr district," and each of them has a permanent district commander. The latter has an adjutant, 3 clerks, and orderlies, per battalion, and a 1st sergeant and 2 other non-commissioned officers per company. These keep the register of the names and addresses of all reserve and landwehr men in their district, also summon, collect and forward them in time of war.

There is a periodical census and registration of all horses in the country, and owners are by law obliged to produce the animals if required, and dispose of them to the government on terms which are settled by a commission. The horses are brought to convenient centres for distribution.

In every district there are store houses where the necessary wagons and harness are kept: also others for articles of clothing camp and garrison equipage. All of these are frequently inspected during the year and kept in good order and repair, and are so arranged in racks that their distribution is very rapid. Similar arrangements exist for the medical and all other departments. Germany and France can mobilize about 20 corps each in 6 days; Russia 22 corps in 14 days; Italy 12 corps in 21 days.

When notice of mobilization is telegraphed to the landwehr districts, every man of the reserve and of the landwehr is at once summoned by notices which are always kept ready, and which state when and where he is to join. These men are formed into detachments and forwarded to their regiments under non-commissioned officers. They there find themselves in the same regiments, battalions and companies in which they formerly received instruction and serving with relatives, friends and fellow townsmen.

While the reservists are joining their regiments the artillery prepares its munition columns, its parks and its depots of reserve munitions, the engineers their bridge equipage, their implement columns, their companies of pontoneers and sappers, their railroad and telegraph sections; the train, its supply columns, its sanitary detachments, its horse depots, ambulances, etc

While, as a whole, the mobilization of a great force seems a "gigantic" undertaking, it is in reality simple, provided the system is decentralized and has been well tested during the leisure of peace conditions. If every corporal, in an army however large, can summon his little command, clothe and equip it,—if every teamster knows where to find his wagon and the harness for its draught animals near at hand, and if, at the same time, the purchasing and supply departments accomplish their work with the same division of labor, the difficulties are reduced to the old element of discipline and vigilance during peace, with a system of inspections which from sheer routine, however, tend to degenerate and become perfunctory. The main thing here as everywhere in the army, is that every individual be convinced, no matter how trivial and petty the work given him may seem, that his part is to do it as well as he can.

Mobilization in the United States —A small standing army recruited by voluntary enlistment may be placed on a strong war footing with much of the facility and promptness peculiar to great military nations. For this, the service should be, first of all, popular, for which reason of many others, the territorial system is indispensable.

Suitable organization is of course prerequisite. A well considered plan* is based on the peace strength recommended by Major General Miles in his annual report, viz., one soldier for each one thousand, or one-tenth of one per cent., of the population. Omitting many details it is as follows:

36 regiments of INFANTRY		36000
14 regiments of CAVALRY		14000
6 batteries of HORSE ARTILLERY at 84 men each	504	
30 batteries of FIELD ARTILLERY at 84 men each	2520	
N. C S. clerks, orderlies, etc., recruiting parties and unassigned recruits for 10 battalions of field and 2 battalions of horse artillery	300	3324
100 batteries of HEAVY ARTILLERY at 75 men each	7500	
Bands, N. C S, artillery mechanics, and other specialists, clerks, orderlies, etc, for organized commands of heavy artillery, and for recruiting parties and unassigned recruits for the heavy artillery	750	8250

* Prof ... y Major H C Hasbrouck, 4th Artillery The details omitted are very complete

4 battalions of engineers at 300 men each	1200	
For band, N. C. S , engineer specialists, clerks, orderlies, etc , and for recruiting parties and unassigned recruits for the engineers	150	1350
Mechanics, clerks, messengers, teamsters and laborers, etc., to be employed in Quartermaster and Subsistence Departments at military posts and stations garrisoned by troops, being about 5% of the combatant strength of the peace establishment		3000
Post N. C. S , the Hospital Corps, Signal Corps, Military Academy detachments, and enlisted men of the Ordnance Department at arsenals and armories		2500
Total enlisted strength on peace footing		68424

INFANTRY REGIMENT, PEACE—ENLISTED STRENGTH.

3 battalions of 4 companies of 75 men each	900
Band, regimental and battalion N C S , etc , recruit detachment, recruiting parties and unassigned recruits	100
Total enlisted strength on peace footing	1000

A 13th and 14th company to be skeletonized and to them to be assigned officers absent on detached service or present for duty with the regimental recruit detachment.

INFANTRY REGIMENT, WAR—ENLISTED STRENGTH.

Each company to be increased to 125 men

The 13th and 14th companies to be organized into a depot battalion for the purpose of collecting, enlisting and instructing men for the service battalions. The President to have the authority to increase the recruits in each depot company to any desired number.

3 service battalions at 500 men each . . . . . :	1500
Regimental N. C. S., etc., 7, battalion N. C. S., etc., 15 . .	22
Total enlisted field strength on war footing	1522

CAVALRY REGIMENT, PEACE—ENLISTED STRENGTH.

3 squadrons of 4 troops of 75 men each	900
Band, regimental and battalion N. C S., etc , recruit detachment, recruiting parties and unassigned recruits	100
Total enlisted strength on peace footing	1000

A 13th and 14th troop to be skeletonized and to them to be assigned officers absent on detached service or present for duty with the regimental recruit detachment.

CAVALRY REGIMENT, WAR—ENLISTED STRENGTH.

Each troop to be increased to 100 men by the addition of 25 privates.

The 13th and 14th troops to be organized into a depot squadron for the purpose of collecting, enlisting, and instructing men for the service squadrons. The President to have the authority to increase the recruits in each depot troop to any desired number.

3 service squadrons at 400 men each	1200
Regimental N C. S , etc., 7, battalion N C. S., etc. 15 . . .	22
Total enlisted field strength on a war footing	1222

LIGHT ARTILLERY, PEACE—ENLISTED STRENGTH.

12 battalions of 3 batteries of 84 men each	3024
Battalion N. C. S, etc , 60 Recruiting parties and 3 recruit detachments including unassigned recruits, 240 . . .	300
Total enlisted strength on peace footing	3324

LIGHT ARTILLERY, WAR--ENLISTED STRENGTH.

Each battery to be increased to 175 men.
The three recruit detachments to be organized into 3 depot batteries for collecting, enlisting, and instructing men for the service batteries and ammunition trains. The President to have the authority to increase the recruits in each depot battery to any desired number.

12 battalions at 525 men each	6300
Battalion N. C. S, etc	65
Total strength of field batteries on war footing	6365

HEAVY ARTILLEY, PEACE—ENLISTED STRENGTH.

The Heavy Artillery to be organized in commands of one or more batteries according to the armament, extent of works to be occupied, and the accessibility of the national guard or volunteer heavy artillery that can be relied upon to aid in the defense.

100 batteries at 75 men each	7500
Bands, Post N C. S., artillery mechanics and specialists assigned to posts and recruit detachments, including unassigned recruits	750
Total enlisted strength heavy artillery on peace footing . . .	8250

HEAVY ARTILLERY, WAR—ENLISTED STRENGTH

Each battery to be increased to 150 men
The recruit detachments to be organized into depot batteries for collecting, enlisting, and instructing men for the service batteries and ammunition trains The President to have the authority to increase the recruits in each depot battery to any desired number.

100 service batteries at 150 men each	15000
Bands, Post N. C. S., etc., artillery specialists and mechanics assigned to posts	500
Total enlisted for service batteries on war footing . . .	15500

ENGINEERS, PEACE.

To consist of 4 battalions of 4 companies each to be organized as recommended by the Chief of Engineers. Two of the battalions to be specially trained in field and siege engineering work, one in pontoon work and one in submarine mining.

ENGINEERS, WAR.

Each company and battalion to be increased to desired strength and a depot battalion organized One battalion of engineers and one pontoon train, to be served by two companies, to be attached to each of the two army corps to be formed. The battalion of submarine miners to be divided into suitable fractions and sent to plant and operate the submarine mines for harbor defense

ARMY SERVICE CORPS AND STAFF DEPARTMENTS ON WAR FOOTING.

"The enlisted men not required for services at posts and permanent stations would furnish a nucleus of well-trained, reliable and disciplined men for the organization of the services of the Quartermaster, Subsistence, and Medical Departments in the field. The additional men needed should be specially enlisted or hired for duty in these departments."

"The proposed peace organization would be sufficiently large for thorough instruction and maintenance of order, and would permit the formation in a short time of two complete Army Corps; each consisting of 27,000 infantry, 90 field guns, a regiment of cavalry, an engineer battalion, pontoon train and ammunition trains. Also two cavalry divisions of six regiments, each division having 6000 men and a battalion of horse artillery. The coast defenses with aid from local national guard and volunteer heavy artillery could be efficiently manned and, the works and guns being provided, the protection of the coast would be assured. The field force would be efficient and reliable, for the new men necessary to bring the peace establishment up to the war footing would be quickly trained and disciplined by close association with the old soldiers. It would be able to at least hold in check any force until time was gained to enlist, organize, and train the necessary volunteers. A sufficient regular force for the first operations of war with any of the great European powers is specially needed. It will take time to organize and train volunteers, but possible adversaries, who are ready for war and have abundant means of ocean transportation, will certainly not allow time for preparation. Too much reliance is placed upon the organized national guard of the several states. These troops are acknowledgedly good and capable of excellent service, but there are many of them who could not leave their business for any considerable length of time without a great sacrifice of personal interests, and these could not give cheerful, willing service during the period necessary to organize the volunteers. Besides this, it is in the national guard that would be found the men, the best and most eager, to officer the volunteers, and almost the only ones in civil life who have the technical knowledge necessary to train them properly. It would be a mistake to employ the national guard infantry, cavalry and field artillery in the first line. Except on occasions of emergency they should be used only for local defense and every facility and encouragement given them to obtain commissions in the volunteers. It is probable that more reliance can be placed upon the service to be obtained from the national guard heavy artillery for local defense than upon the other arms of the same force for distant field service."

"To organize the regular army for war service, the companies, troops, and batteries would be increased to their war strength, and the recruiting depots to keep them full would be established. The 36 infantry regiments would be organized into 12 brigades of three regiments each, the 12 brigades into 4 divisions, the 4 divisions into 2 army corps. To each division to be assigned one battalion of field artillery for the divisional artillery, and to each corps 3 battalions for the corps artillery. To each army corps to be assigned one regiment of cavalry, one squadron being attached to each division, and one kept under the immediate orders of the corps commander each division and corps commander would then have the facilities for information, security and reconnoitering in the vicinity of his command. One battalion of engineers and a pontoon train to be served by two engineer companies to be attached to each corps. 12 regiments of cavalry to be organized into 4 brigades of 3 regiments each, the 4 brigades into 2 cavalry divisions of 2 brigades each. One battalion of horse artillery to be attached to each division."

"The divisional and corps ammunition trains to be officered by surplus officers of the light and heavy artillery and manned by non-commissioned officers and men furnished by the artillery depots."

"The necessary vehicles and harness for the ammunition and supply trains to be kept in store ready for use."

"The proposed organization of the infantry is recommended because the 3 battalions for a regiment, the 3 regiments for a brigade and 3 brigades for the largest battle unit, the division, permits two thirds of the force to be employed in the fighting line with its local supports and reserves and the remaining third to be used as a general reserve. The proposed organization for the cavalry regiments and brigades offers the same advantages for dismounted fire action and permits the ready formation into three lines for mounted action."

"A scheme should be prepared and altered from time to time to meet changed conditions for the mobilization, command, and staff of each brigade, division and corps, and for the organization of the recruiting depots, the ammunition and supply trains. The number of clerks and orderlies for brigade and higher headquarters, and the source from which these men are to be obtained, should be determined. The organization of the companies, troops, batteries, battalions, regiments, and recruit depots for the volunteers should be the same as that prescribed for the regular army. Time would be gained and possible errors of hasty legislation avoided, if regulations, based on Act of Congress, are provided for the organization of volunteers to be raised, for their subsistence and quarters until mustered, and for their muster into service."

The scheme of mobilization which this organization contemplates and admits of, while it would be practicable under many circumstances, would be greatly facilitated as to *economy in time and expense* by permanency of station and the localization of commands. These two advantages are paramount, but there are others which are very striking.

1st. Because of the bond of sympathy which would exist between the troops and the community in which they were permanently stationed and which would furnish the young men to the ranks. These would be under home influences during their whole term of service; they could visit their homes with short furloughs and at small expense, cases of misconduct would be known and disparaged by a public opinion which the soldier had been accustomed to respect, while promotion for good conduct and attention to duty would become doubly valuable. In a few years the pride of the community in its regiment and the pride of the regiment in its locality would build up a wonderful morale and esprit de corps, and troops from adjacent sections would compete in creating and upholding honorable traditions of service.

2nd. Because of the ease and economy with which the ranks could be kept filled in time of peace and recruited to the war strength if hostilities threatened. At present the United States army is absolutely divorced from the people at large and the officer or soldier is like an alien when away from his post in uniform, albeit the country has no better or more loyal citizens. With commands localized in populous communities in which disbursements for supplies would generally be made, the large posts and barracks would be visited by civilians in all stations of life, who would be impressed with the good order, system, cleanliness and humane and wholesome displine of the service; and who would be quick to notice physical and mental improvement in friends and acquaintances. It would be apparent that the soldier has comforts and means assured him, which are often wanting in civil life and that the army is in no respects a Botany Bay for unruly characters. After his tour of service he would go back to the community, where his ingrained habits would be of incalculable use to him at home, in business and in the militia. His example and advice would induce others to follow in his footsteps and these, in turn, others, until, in many places, boys would look forward to the army as a career or to entering it as they would enter any other school for a term of years. If war threatened, the enthusiasm and martial spirit which is then always rife, would supply recruits in ample number, for these would join relatives, friends and fellow townsmen, in place of being drafted to distant commands to serve with strangers. There would be available a self established reserve, of men who had served with the colors, most of them within convenient distance for promptly joining their old commands.

It is hardly necessary to point out that the extent of the United States, with its varieties of climate, productions and material interests, has in some quarters a tendency to create sectional differences and prejudices which in time may loosen the attachment of one section or another to the general government. A popular army will introduce a leaven of loyalty and devotion to the flag as nothing else can.

3rd. Because of the acquaintance which would spring up and increase between army and militia, to the professional benefit of both. Under the system of frequent changes of station the militia, officers and men, no sooner feel at home at the nearest military station, than the entente cordiale has to be renewed, if at all, under difficulties and with strangers Permanent garrisons mean that the personnel of the militia will ultimately form, essentially, a part of them in professional work and social recreation.

4th. Because in every part of the country there will be some troops thoroughly familiar with the terrain and, in case of invasion, a few troops at least who will be fighting literally for their firesides and homes. In case of sea-coast artillery troops, these cannot be too familiar with the harbor which they may be called upon to defend: to remove them from time to time to other places is a shortsighted and indefensible policy.

5th. Because the supplies necessary for the complete equipment of the "reserve" must be stored, inspected and kept in good order at the large stations. if they are destined for the organizations serving there and not for unknown troops who may sooner or later come after, an interest, however selfish, will be taken in maintaining them at the highest standard.

VI.

Concentration.—Immediately after mobilization is completed the work of moving the forces and massing them near the frontier of the state to be attacked, begins. Concentration may therefore be divided into two periods: the transport of troops and their strategic deployment.

The region in which the troops are massed, from whence they will advance or in which they may await attack is called the zone of concentration. It has been selected in advance of war, according to the character of the frontiers, but is subject to modification by the duration of the enemy's mobilization and by the strategic significance of his first movements thereafter.

In concentration the massing of the forces must be protected from interference by the enemy, and threatened home provinces must be covered. Skillful selection and occupation of a zone should result in doing both.

"It is certain, indeed, that if the assemblements of a grand army take place upon the flank of the probable direction of the enemy's columns, the latter will be forced to abandon his projects.'

"The assemblement of the different parts of an army cannot, without danger, be effected under the eyes of the enemy and exposed to his blows. The army is then obliged to conceal its movements behind a protecting screen formed by troops, obstacles of the ground, or a combination of both "*

"*Mistakes made at the outset, in the assemblement of the armies, cannot be repaired during the entire course of the campaign.*"

Inversely, it is true that the general who succeeds in massing his troops betimes in a zone of concentration rightly chosen, already controls the situation. He may go forward confident that thereafter the best line of conduct will be made plain to him from day to day by the course of events. Even if defeated in battle the defeat will be inflicted under circumstances which are, relatively, the most favorable for him.

Strategy, therefore, has no concern with any operation nearly so important as concentration. It is equally true that the size of modern armies is imposed by railroads,† i. e., by the number of soldiers that may be transported to the frontier and kept supplied

---

* Derrécagaix
† As the size of modern cannon is imposed by improved powder.

and in a state of efficiency. Here the connection between strategy and logistics is very close

Principles of transport. General considerations. "First of all, provision should be made for the wants of the troops during the period of transportation. On account of the positive rule which prescribes that the troops shall be transported first,—the different arms of the service being apportioned according to the exigencies of the situation,—and that the provision trains shall be held back until the last, it must be calculated that the units disembarking during the first days will not receive their supplies of provisions in less than a week. As to the local resources, it is estimated that the richest sections can furnish these troops subsistence for no longer a period than two days. Abundant supplies must, therefore, be collected near the zone of concentration either before the actual declaration of war or during the period of mobilization"

Transport by rail. "The concentration is of such importance that the loss of a single hour should not be looked upon as a matter of trifling consideration. The greatest possible number of railroads should, therefore, be called into requisition"

"The influence of these roads upon the movements of armies now becomes all-controlling. It is understood that if each army corps had an independent double track at its disposal for the transportation of its various elements to the frontier, if it were stationed upon this line, and so mobilized as to ensure uninterrupted use of its means of transport, the concentration would be effected under the most favorable circumstances. Finally, if at the terminal stations the sidings were sufficiently numerous to allow the trains to succeed one another every 15 minutes, 96 trains could be unloaded in 24 hours. It would thus be possible to secure the arrival of the 105 trains of an army corps in $26\frac{1}{4}$ hours."*

The great military powers have endeavored to so construct their railroads in number and direction that this perfection of result may be approximated On the frequency with which trains can be dispatched rather than on the speed of these, depends the number of troops which may be transported in a given time: in any case, therefore, it is necessary to have a number of disembarking stations on each line at convenient intervals and within supporting distance of each other.

Military nations have a railway section of the General Staff (apart from the Supply Department or Railway Troops proper)

* Derrecagaix

whose duty it is to follow everything that affects the subject of military transport, and to possess an accurate knowledge of all railway systems at home and abroad, together with the amount of traffic they are capable of, and work out large military transport arrangements. When railway lines pass suddenly from ordinary traffic to transport large bodies of troops and munitions of war great confusion will ensue unless proper measures are taken beforehand to avert it. In 1870 the French had no such system, and as this was their first experience in transporting and supplying large bodies of troops confusion soon resulted. Early in the war 7000 railway carriages were blocked together in a solid mass at Metz. It is easy to understand that, even on several tracks, these extended for miles. The supplies, food, ammunition, arms, clothing, medicines, pontoons, wagons, were urgently needed, yet no one knew what any one carriage contained, and, opened at random, it was found that many contained an assortment of miscellaneous stores. In this case, want of system and management rendered the railways an absolute disadvantage. There was telegraphing to and fro, the officers in despair the men murmuring and insubordinate, new trains constantly arriving and the enemy advancing like a black cloud from the horizon.

In addition to keeping up supplies of all kinds railways are necessary to remove the sick and wounded and especially to keep up the effective strength of the army at the front. In active campaign the yearly losses will be 50% under most favorable conditions and will usually reach 70% to 75%. At the end of the first month about one-eighth of the yearly loss must be forwarded and thereafter one-tenth to one-twelfth. In addition to these, special reinforcements are sent after a battle.*

Special considerations.—Whether a distinct advantage will be gained in point of time by sending troops by rail should be carefully considered. It will often accelerate concentration, if only by disembarrassing a terminus of troops with which it is overcrowded, to direct them by marching to some other station towards the point of concentration, where return carriages may meet them. For short distances no time is gained in moving large forces by rail, as the time required for entraining and detraining and the interval of time between trains and delays which are incidental to railroads and cannot be foreseen,

---

* A European estimate of the annual loss of infantry in campaign, is that of the cavalry and artillery. In future wars the casualties among men greater than it will be well fought, disencumbered of lances and trappings, are the arm they will suffer from improved shrapnel and be decimated if it attempts to "go in" to some of its more

will counteract the advantages due to rapidity of transit. This simple consideration was unaccountably overlooked on several occasions by the French in 1870. Canrobert, ordered with over 30,000 men, horses, &c., from Chalons to Metz, a four or five days march, took about that length of time to entrain. He could have been in Metz with the whole of his troops on the day when his last trains were leaving Chalons. There were other instances quite as striking.

This matter has been clearly stated* as follows:

"In calculating the net gain of time by transporting masses of troops by rail the following factors should be kept in mind:"

1. "The number of trains which can be loaded within a given time; this again depends on the number of entraining stations, the rapidity with which the rolling stock can be collected at these points and the time required for entraining the troops."

2. "The rapidity with which troops can be disembarked and with which the detraining stations can be cleared of troops and empty trains."

3 "The interval of time which the considerations of safety require to be observed between successive trains."

"Taking as a basis the figures obtaining for a German army corps at the outbreak of the Franco-Prussian war we have"

"The corps requires 92 trains of from 50 to 60 cars; 18 trains are despatched per day, making 360 miles in 24 hours; this distance will bring a corps to almost any frontier in Germany. The embarkation will last a little more than five days, i. e., the last troops would embark on the 6th day, arrive and disembark at the terminal station 360 miles distant on the 7th day. The whole corps would begin active operations on the 8th day; it would have traversed a distance in 24 hours which would require 24 foot marches at the high average rate of 15 miles per day and without any days of rest. The net gain would be 17 days."†

"Were the distance to be traversed but 15 miles, the corps would cover it in one day by foot march, while by rail it would take seven days, a loss of six days. To ensure gain of time by transport of masses by rail, requires therefore that the distance to be traversed bear a certain ratio to the number of troops."

As a rule this ratio will be best determined by the traffic managers of the roads, in consultation with the commandant of the forces. The officials of the railroads in the United States and Canada are men of uncommon practical ability and entirely

---

* By Lieutenant Carl Reichmann, 4th U S Infantry.
† The number of days stated has since been greatly reduced

trustworthy. As many of the details as possible may safely be left to them.

The accumulation of rolling stock at stations requires time and the first days after declaration of war or after war is known to be inevitable will be devoted to this and to completion and concentration of small bodies ready at their garrisons to be marched to points of entraining. The concentration of large bodies, such as an army corps, is not advisable, previous to their transport It is also best to complete the concentration of a unit on the frontier,—at least a division, rather than parts of several, and to do this complete organizations must arrive in rapid succession. Thus a full regiment with its regimental transport, ready for a campaign of any length will be entrained and protect the concentration of its brigade, the other organizations of which follow promptly. To do this it is necessary to prepare careful time tables in advance and to test them frequently in time of peace.

Railway troops. Continental armies have battalions of railway troops intended to form in war the nucleus of the military railway forces, and in peace to train men and officers. A railway battalion is divided into constructing and working companies. The first make improvised lines, the second take them in hand as soon as made, man them with engineers, firemen and personnel generally. The service, once established, is handed over to the civil staff, the trained companies moving on to complete another section.

General Sherman pronounced against the formation of a special railway corps for the United States, probably recalling the efficient services rendered during the War of Secession by the railroad corps which was quickly and easily organized mainly of mechanics and railroad men. Yet General McCullum,* the military superintendent of railroads showed in his report that the railroad corps used with such success in 1864, was the result of the experience gained in 1862 and 1863; in other words that the practical training of two years was required to create a corps d' elite. The United States can, however, afford to neglect this matter during peace with impunity, while other nations cannot. Apart from the army of trained employees which numberless

---

* An architect and engineer, appointed superintendent of all the railroads in the United States, with full power to appropriate them with all their appurtenances for the public use and with positive orders to be ready at all times to execute any order instant on is first given He at once organized a strong military administration certering in his w.. of the largest system of railroads in the world and created a quasi military corps c . neers, skilled mechanics and laborers.

roads render necessary and who all have the keen, practical sense peculiar to their nationality, nearly everyone else has a familiarity with railroads and their working. The trains are open from end to end, the public as a rule, is not excluded from stations, sidings, yards and shops, the track passes through the center of populous towns and is a highway for pedestrians, and everywhere in the country people have taken a personal interest from childhood up in railroads which their communities have helped to construct In Europe opposite conditions obtain in every respect.*

Indeed, as far as ability is concerned to call promptly into existence and to organize a corps of railroad troops, the United States has an advantage over most other nations which is unique. A measure of their efficiency can be best obtained by citing, in general, what they accomplished in the last last two years of the civil war, when the actual running of trains and transport of troops over thousands of miles of rail were the easiest of their tasks

"As an illustration of the nature and magnitude of the work accomplished in the military division of the Mississippi alone in supplying General Sherman's army, it may be mentioned that there were laid or relaid 433 miles in length of track. There were built or rebuilt over eighteen miles in length of bridges. There were in use 260 locomotives and 3,383 cars. There were employed 17,035 men and the whole expenses reached the enormous sum of $29,662,781. It would not be difficult to multiply examples; a better and more satisfactory idea of the importance of the department and of the actual part it played in the war, may be gathered from a perusal of the following figures: At one time there were employed in the department 34,964 men. From first to last we operated 2,105 miles of road and made use of 419 locomotives and 6,330 cars. Of bridges we built in all over 26 miles. The expenses of the department are scarcely less suggestive. They reach the high figure of $42,462,145."†

Railways were constructed at the rate of a mile per day, including grading· where a road had been destroyed, reconstruction was much more rapid,—so rapid that the enemy often found it profitable to interfere with traffic by obstructions, switching out a rail, firing on trains, &c. The railroad bridge over the Etowah, 625 feet long and 75 feet high, was rebuilt in 6 days, and one equally long but only half as high, in less than two.

---

* This seems to be a good example of a number of cases where American and European conditions are at variance American officers who are disturbed at what seem off-hand methods and at the apparent neglect of matters which are thought vital in Europe, should consider these differences well before advocating changes

In 1865, Schofield's corps of about 18,000 was moved from Tennessee to the North Carolina coast to co-operate with Sherman. Within 5 days from the receipt of the order the troops, baggage, wagons, animals &c. were concentrated at various landings on the Tennessee and Ohio rivers, from which they were taken in boats to the railroads, and then by rail to their destination—a move of 1400 miles, in the midst of winter in 11 days without accident. Every train was composed, one half of cars with seats and one half of box-cars with straw. At certain stations along the road hot coffee was prepared in advance, with which the soldiers filled their canteens and then exchanged places in the cars,— those who had occupied seats going to the box cars to sleep.

Entraining and detraining. These matters are regulated in all services, especially as regards field batteries and horses: the regulations may be consulted at any time and need no recapitulation. To load a field battery on flat cars and the horses in horse-cars is said to require one-half an hour, but it has frequently been done in the United States service in 15 minutes without previous practice. Infantry can board the cars anywhere along the line and need no platforms. It is not well to confuse the men with instructions, the main thing is that all officers, from the regimental commander down, be present, that absolute quiet and good order be preserved and idlers and spectators be excluded or kept at a distance. European carriages are filled and emptied of foot troops more readily than the American cars. The latter should be entered simultaneously at both ends, the first men entering taking the first seats next the door, to the right and left without obstructing the passage (while removing their knapsacks and accoutrements) and filling the car towards the middle. When the car is full, an officer should direct the removal of knapsacks and accoutrements and see that they are stowed properly· he can then do valuable service, however uncongenial, by remaining in the car throughout the journey.

The ordinary water tanks in American cars are entirely inadequate for the needs of troops and a barrel of water should be placed by the railroad officials in each car. The officials are also apt to leave lamps uncared for. once under way neglects on the part of the company in this and other respects are difficult to correct. darkness adds especially to the discomfort of travelling in a crowded car.

The number of trains that can be despatched in war. from one station in a given time seems to be greater in the United States than in Europe where 20 trains per day was a fair average. On two occasions the French moved large bodies of troops in trains running at 10 minutes interval. The question is entirely one of sufficiency of equipment on the part of the roads and celerity of handling the troops, and it is impossible to formulate general rules which may be always trusted These may apply to the great trunk lines, but where several lines are included in the route, unforseen delays are apt to be numerous. Ordinary break-downs, wash-outs and interruptions from many other causes are of daily occurance in peace traffic and they will occur more often when trains are running at short intervals with new time tables. Delays in entraining troops will be reduced to a minimum if all officers, including those of the highest rank are present and leave no part of the work to subordinates or staff-officers. Under the usual conditions it is within limits to assume that from 90,000 to 100,000 men, with horses, wagons and supplies can be moved 250 miles in 24 hours.*

Destruction of railroads. Railroads may be crippled, i. e., rendered useless for a time, but they cannot be destroyed. In mountainous sections where there are many tunnels and viaducts traffic may be interrupted for an indefinite period by destroying these, but this kind of road is exceptional. European troops carry a demolition equipment with dynamite cartridges, with which to destroy the fine solid bridges, viaducts, &c., which are common there. The more rapid methods of the American war, where they are applicable, are more serviceable because the time necessary for undisturbed work is often wanting.

A sufficient number of men all on the same side of the road can pry under sleepers and rails, and at the word of command raise track sleepers and all and overturn it bodily Rails are then detached from the sleepers, the latter piled crib fashion in piles 4 or 5 feet high and bundles of rails laid across, weighted at the ends. The cribs being fired the rails become red hot in the middle and are bent by the end weights. This is a very rapid method, but the road can be quickly restored because the rails can be straightened on the spot very easily. If there is time each rail is taken, when red hot in the middle, and bent against and as far as possible around a tree or telegraph pole; or a lateral twist may be given it by applying leverage in opposite directions at the ends. These methods are comparatively slow

---

* The General Manager of the Baltimore and Ohio railroad states that 350 ro troops fully equipped and supplied, could be moved from the interior of the United States to the seacoast 1000 miles in 4 hours by four trunk lines, without interfering materially with the ordinary traffic of the country At the United States Infantry and Cavalry School, it is taught that trains should not be despatched from a station with less interval than 10 minutes. * * * 10, 16 passenger cars constitute a train and run 20, 30 miles per hour '

but are very effective, as rails properly twisted must be sent to the rolling mill.

With adequate protection and precautions a long line of railroad may be kept in running order in spite of an unremitting succession of raids against it. "The energy displayed in repairing the line will discourage the enemy, who will soon come to recognize the futility of wasting much time and labor with no lasting results."

Administration.—As a means for concentrating armies within striking distance of the theatre of war railroads must be under military administration· as a means for supplying these armies while operating in the theatre of war, they should be under civil administration. As both conditions exist at the same time there must be between them a line of demarkation which is called the transfer line, with its transfer stations. As the army advances new transfer lines are selected, the older lines becoming secondary depots. In rear of this line the administration is civil because there should be no interference with the regular traffic of the country or the supply of its productions on which the army depends. At the same time it is obvious that for a certain distance in rear of the army there should be absolute military control regulating the distribution.

In the Franco-German war the Rhine was for some time the transfer line, Mayence, Mannheim and Coblenz being the transfer stations. Subsequently the line was moved to the Moselle and afterwards to the Meuse.

Deployment.—"The troops having reached termini and disembarked, it is essential to consider their further disposition. To leave them at the landing places is impossible. They must be established to the front in such a way as to be able to support each other in case of need. Hence the necessity of making several marches, generally short, after disembarking, the effect of which will be to place each division upon the points it is to provisionally occupy. With the transport, this completes the concentration of the forces upon a frontier zone, and is equally subject to rules. The strategic deployment is designed to put the army in condition for immediate service."

"The cantonments should be chosen so that the army may be able to undertake the first marches as soon as possible, sometimes even before the transport is completed. Their localities will be dictated by the roads upon which the corps must advance toward the enemy's frontier. The certainty of being able to take the initiative will give the power of extending the deployment. The contrary would be the case if an offensive movement on the part of the enemy was feared."

"Once the deployment is ended, each army will occupy a certain number of frontier posts constituting its front. The direction of this front with reference to the enemy's lines of operation, is not a matter of indifference, it should vary according to circumstances. In principle, it is so ordered as to be prepared for all contingencies, while, if possible, threatening the adversary's line of communications. In every case, the first condition of success for a deployment as well as for a concentration, is security. Hence arises the necessity for double precaution."

"In the first instance, to protect the frontier against the enemy's incursions during the period of mobilization; then, to cover the concentration."

"At the moment war is declared, the protection of the territory devolves entirely upon the garrisons nearest the enemy But immediately afterwards, or at the same time, if possible, a defensive screen should be organized, capable, by its strength and the extent of its front, of allowing the various bodies to assemble and to support each other in case of attack. Hence arises the obligation of sending to the front strong masses of cavalry reinforced by artillery and supported in rear, if circumstances require it, by a large infantry unit."

"This duty is a feature of the reconnaissance service of the independent cavalry divisions. To cover the concentration is, however, only a part of the service they are called upon to render. They must, in addition, seek to retard the union of the enemy's forces. Eight or ten brigades of cavalry, each accompanied by a battery, throwing themselves unexpectedly upon the enemy's territory, on the day following the declaration of war, would burn his magazines and destroy his railroads, detraining stations and other important works, spreading terror among the inhabitants for sixty leagues from the frontier, and at one blow arresting mobilization and concentration."

"Whatever may be the difficulties presented by a concentration, this truth must be understood, that the strategic deployment of an army is the only act of war that depends completely upon the will of the supreme directing power The combinations connected with it, however complicated they may be, are not under the control of outside circumstances. It is later only that chance comes into play to put a hand upon the course of events."

"The general principles, then, which, though not absolute in their character, greatly facilitate the concentration of armies, are as follows.

1st. Before the concentration, *assemblement near the disembarking stations, of provisions sufficient to supply the army,* at least during the entire period of transportation,

2nd. *Protection of the frontier,* from the day war is declared, by the first disposable troops,

3rd. *Dispatch to the frontier of the first mobilized units, for the purpose of covering the strategic deployment,*

4th. *Distribution of the corps and division upon the zone of concentration,* in order more or less close (generally echelon) according to the probable character of the first combats,

5th *Concentration of the armies upon angular fronts,* when the circumstances are favorable for such a direction."*

The first movements after concentration will lead to collisions, if the concentration was faulty the forces will not be at places where they are available. "Where the opposing forces are equal such errors will in most cases effect the retreat of the one and the advance of the other." "It is easy to perceive the connection of the seven defeats, which were inflicted upon France in the first period of the great war, with the original dispositions affecting the massing of the troops."

Marching.—After troops are detrained their first marches begin and it is desirable that, for the first two or three days, these should be short, though increasing in length from day to day. After a long journey by rail, troops are very unfit and nothing will be gained, while much may be lost by a long initial march, even if over good roads with favorable weather.

Rate. Everyone knows that, including short rests, the average rate of marching is for infantry, 2¾, 3 miles, for field artillery 4 miles and for cavalry and horse artillery 4, 5 miles, per hour. But this is for small bodies of troops under favorable conditions of roads and weather. The rate is affected:

1st. The rate for the field artillery is almost always, and that for the cavalry and horse artillery often, limited to that of the infantry.

2nd. The rate decreases rapidly with the size of the force. Under normal conditions a division will average 2¼ to 2½ miles, and a corps only 2 miles per hour.

3rd. Weather affects the rate apart from its effect on the roads Heat reduces it. excessive heat, especially with dust,

---
* Condensed from Derrécagaix

may reduce it practically to zero.* Stong head winds retard a march greatly as do, also, driving rain storms, while a gentle rain is often of service. Cold weather, even if severe, accelerates the rate of marching.

4th. The condition of the roads predominates as a co-efficient of the rate. They may be more or less dusty, sandy, muddy, slippery, icy, swampy (as in the Gulf States, where many miles of improvised corduroy had often to be laid), or cut up generally. It is hardly an alleviation to have stretches of good and bad road alternating. In the War of Secession the roads were never good; they were sometimes fair; they were usually vile. Marching and manoeuvring on exterior lines of vast extent, these roads were a most formidable obstacle. At the other extreme stand the fine highroads of Europe, on many of which two columns in route can march abreast, the unfenced fields on either side being frequently passable for mounted troops. It is impossible to overestimate the effect of bad roads it extends from a considerable retardation all the way to infinity, i. e., the rate of march may become zero. One day during the pursuit of Hood's forces after Nashville, a body of Federal troops took the road in the early morning, only to lie about in the same place all day, and return in the evening to their bivouac of the night before. Good roads are much cut up by the passage of troops, bad roads become rapidly worse and add to the difficulties of the rearmost troops, already beset by disadvantages of their position in column.

5th The rate decreases with the number of miles marched, the decrease being very perceptible after the second hour. It is difficult for an average man, walking alone, to make 5 miles per hour. 4 miles is rapid walking, but practicable; 8 miles in 2 hours is impossible without continuous effort or special capacity. The rate is greatest, everything else being equal, in the early morning. it decreases as the day advances· troops starting in the afternoon are already tired, in a measure, from lounging about camp. This is another disadvantage for troops in rear.

The head of the column should start at early dawn, as soon as it is light enough to distinguish the road †

Rests and elongation. The necessity for rests reduces the

---

* In the summer of 1864 marching in the Gulf States the writer arrived in bivouac one afternoon with one other officer and the colors the rest of the regiment, including the mounted officers, were prostrated—the Colonel, permanently disabled by sun-stroke The division of 1... or 12, x men was temporarily broken up and scattered along the road for 10 or 12 miles To march troops under such conditions is an absurdity

† The writer it is fair to state is here at variance with others and perhaps with regulations His personal experience in marching has, however, been exceptionally great and

aggregate of miles. Rests are intimately connected with the elongation or tailing off of a column. After marching an hour a rest of 10 minutes is allowed. This is longer than necessary but is obligatary for the foremost troops because those in rear will get less. After the third hour, or when the march is about three-fifths completed, allow a full half hour for all the troops.

In marching the depth of the column increases up to a certain maximum, this maximum varying with the condition of the roads, with the drill and discipline of the troops and even with their nationality and morale. The original cause of this "tailing off" is, perhaps, difficult to trace: it may start with individual soldiers throughout the column who want and take more room than the drill regulations give them or who pick their footing with undue care at any rate it is inevitable and unavoidable. It is also exceedingly inconvenient. To lessen it, the Germans drill their infantry, almost to excess, in marching while keeping distances. That they are not entirely successful, Prince Hohenlohe may testify, when he refers to 1870 war experience and says: "Anyone who has ever made a march of this kind knows how disagreeable, trying and wearisome these checks are on the march, when at every moment each man, enveloped in thick dust and with his nose jammed against the pack of the man in front of him, has perpetually to halt, not knowing whether it is worth while to 'order his arms.' even though the words 'order arms' be given, he must still, at the command 'right shoulder,' take up his rifle again and march on." The amount of elongation will vary greatly with its functions which are many, mainly the state of the roads, the strength of the column, the drill, discipline and morale of the troops and, as already stated, with their national characteristics. also with their physical condition.

The connection between rests and elongation is, of course, this Whenever a body of troops halts, those in rear close up to drill-book distances,—but if at the hourly halt of 10 minutes, the elongation has been so great that it will take those in rear about that long to close up they will have no rest at all. It therefore becomes necessary to designate a march unit, which shall march and halt independently and the size of which may vary with the functions of elongation referred to For practical purposes these may all be eliminated excepting the state of the roads. It will then be the duty of the commanding officer of each march unit to keep his proper distance from the rear of the unit immediately preceding him, and to halt at the proper time for rests To do this, all must have watches set to a common standard with which they must be frequently compared.

On normal marches of 5 to 6 hours duration troops march one hour and then rest 10 minutes. at the end of the third hour they rest about 45 minutes.

It is desirable and indeed necessary that the march unit correspond with the unit of command, and the latter must be small enough for the mounted chief at its head to observe and control the distance which he is required to keep. Taking the depth of a three battalion regiment of 1200 men at about 530 yards and the rate of march at 3 miles per hour, the following table may be constructed:

Roads	Tailing	Elongation.	Rear men close up in	Rear men rest.
Fine	⅙	65 yds.	45 s	9 m 15 s
Good	¼	132 yds.	1 m. 30 s	8 m 30 s
Fair	⅓	198 yds.	2 m. 15 s.	7 m 45 s
Bad	½	264 yds.	3 m.	. 7 m.

It will be seen from this that if the regiment is taken as a march unit the rearmost men will have 7 minutes rest even on bad roads. If the roads are very bad, i. e., if the elongation exceeds two-thirds, the wagons alone will so delay the march that any system will be impossible and it will then be necessary to allow each company commander or even each chief of squad to make what progress he can, retaining as well as may be his place in column A march under these circumstances will throw the best command out of gear.

If, then, the grouping which answers to a halt of 10 minutes is the regiment of infantry, or a number of carriages of an equivalent extent, every regiment which will form the head of a column, will maintain as nearly as possible the prescribed pace, and will make a halt of 10 minutes at the end of every hour's march. "In this case an extreme regularity is indispensible. Every day the chief of the column gives the indications of the march" (i. e., allows for, or permits, a certain amount of tailing) "and every chief of a group should apply them rigorously. Nothing is more simple than to insert, in the order of movement, the indication of the time of the first hourly halt Everyone knows that the pause is for 10 minutes, that they ought to march for an hour, neither more nor less, and traverse during that time a certain distance. That being well known the fractions will of their own accord make successive halts at the same hour, and the this but what is very practical, with watches regulated every day."

"There remains only to determine the distances to take at starting off between the heads of groups, and to preserve these integrally during the whole march. They will be one-eighth or one-fourth of the length of the group, at the least, and sometimes much more. A good method of marching, rigorously applied, will undoubtedly restrain the losses of distance in a very sensible manner. The chief of the column should take account of the prolongation of his troops by attentive and sustained observations during the first days of the march. According to the results obtained he will modify his instructions, so as to approach his groups as much as possible without ever closing them so as to deprive them of the necessary elasticity."

If, for example, the elongation is allowed at one-half.

Regiment in column . . . . 530 yards
Elongation . . . . 265 yards
Distance between regiments . . . . 40 yards

Total . . . . 835 yards

the leading guide of the second regiment will be kept at about 835 yards from the guide of the first, and it should be made one of the special duties of a mounted staff officer to maintain him at that distance, as nearly as possible. He can do this sometimes by the eye alone, if he is a practical judge of distances, but more generally he must occasionally estimate and check the distance by time. Being mounted he can frequently notice when the head of the regiment in front passes a conspicuous object near the road: in the case in point the head of his own regiment should pass this point between 9 and 10 minutes later.

To start the march in the morning an initial point is designated in advance of the bivouac the evening before and the order for the march must designate the precise hour and minute when the head of each march unit will pass it. The commandant of each unit will have caused the ground between this point and his bivouac to be reconnoitered, and in passing it he will compare his watch with that of the staff officer stationed there. The latter will have orderlies whom he can despatch in time to hasten any organization which appears to be tardy.

It may be well to say that the method which has just been sketched does not work as smoothly under conditions of active service as the description indicates, especially for the first few days, but even an approach to accuracy soon develops a system immeasurably superior to what may be termed the "go as you please" methods which formerly obtained. It requires unceasing vigilance and hard work on the part of all officers, especially of the mounted officers and aids but it is a great misfortune for the troops and indirectly for their leader, if on this account and because of occasional friction, it be allowed to fall into disuse. Aids are furnished with horses on the march and are enabled to live with comparative comfort in camp. This enables them— and is intended to enable them—to do work on the march which is of infinite value and which no other officers can do as well because of other duties which demand attention.

Marches require zealous, expert and tireless supervision. The most brilliant conceptions, the soundest plans, the strategist and tactician alike must fail, if troops do not move over the prescribed distance and do not arrive where they are wanted in good condition. Ragged troops fight well* and hungry troops, if not weakened by privation, fight well also, foot-sore and weary troops who have been jerked along the roads to cover a certain number of miles, are worthless.

During the War of Secession it often happened that little or no attention was paid to the proper marching of troops. The frequent want of success in isolated and subordinate operations of the Federal forces can, it is believed, be generally traced to this neglect; and the aggregate of failures reacted to upset one combination after another. The Federals operated on exterior lines, over an immense territory, always difficult, sometimes a wilderness The most obvious considerations should have suggested the necessity for closing in on their well led and brave adversary behind his breastworks, with elastic troops, hardened and trained by systematic handling. As a rule, however, the matter of systematic marching was neglected, and harrassed and tired troops were hurried into line at the sound of the guns in front. So true is this, that men often welcomed the indications of a fight, in that it withdrew them for a time from the roads to the woods and fields, where lying down awaiting orders, it was nothing uncommon for them to fall asleep under fire

There is one thing which the General in command, and he alone, can do under any circumstances His strategy may be at fault, his tactics left to subordinates to execute, his supplies insufficient or tardy: he can march his troops properly,—march them so that each day will be an improvement in that the men

---
* Ragged troops for some inscrutable reason, have always fought well Anglo-Saxons, at least, fight better before, than after dinner

will be gaining by systematic training in the open. He can surround himself with staff officers imbued with this idea even if they can neither read nor write, and he can see to it personally that they carry out its demands If the road has obstacles they must be removed in time, and if it takes long to do this the troops will rather be left in camp than attempt to make 5 or 10 miles by irregular forward movements. Excepting the hourly and noon-day halts none must occur without ascertaining promptly their probable duration and notifying subdivisions at once by preconcerted signals passed rapidly down the column. Where heads of march units and others responsible for its conduct do not attend strictly to their duties, penalties for neglect should be imposed without exception and without mercy.

No march should be undertaken without every soldier knowing its probable length, and, if possible, none so late that any considerable number of troops will reach camp after dark. Whatever be the hour named for the start the troops must not be aroused sooner than necessary. In this connection there is sometimes a tendency on the part of subordinates to make assurance doubly sure. Thus the commander-in-chief will designate the start for 4 a. m., his leading corps commander, to be sure, for 3:30 a m. division commanders, for the same reason, for 3 a. m., and brigade and regimental commanders for a still earlier hour In all of these cases, and in all others connected with the march the higher commanders and their aids must be ubiquitous and indefatigable, whatever the hour of day or night. There is an ever present, strong temptation, especially where everyone is fagged out during a protracted campaign, to cling, or get back, to the camp fire or tent and not to miss the hot meal which is known to be in waiting and which 8 or 9 hours in the open air has made very inviting

"You would scarcely believe how easily a mounted officer forgets the amount of exertion required from a dismounted man, above all, if the officer has never himself marched on foot during a campaign. There is an abyss between the comfort of the one and the discomfort of the other," who, in addition, at the end of his march goes on outpost duty or fatigue, or finds what sleep he can on the ground in the rain.

The greatest amelioration of marches are the rests. Men look forward to the hourly rests of only 5 or 10 minutes with absolute pleasure. The midday rest may be an hour or longer. A whole day's rest every few days is recommended in the books, but this is often not practicable and is of doubtful value. Marching gets to be a habit or a knack, like keeping in 'training, and men look forward to the end of the day's march as they do, in a lesser degree, to the end of the hourly spurts, while they will spend a whole day lying about in the open fields with something like impatience. . It is better to shorten the daily marches a little. Still, occasional halts of a day are necessary that troops may wash their underclothing, bathe, sew on buttons and make repairs generally. If troops seem tired the halts should be lengthened without lessening the pace: a uniform, swinging gait is always the best.

After all has been said, every march is a case by itself, requiring special care on the part of the officers These must familiarize themselves as nearly as possible with the features of the road and country Defiles, bridges, hills, bad places in the roads and the like, all obstruct a march, and there are always unforseen circumstances which arise to interrupt the smoothness of a march as it is ordered on paper. The standing orders for marches, of Major-General Crawford as issued to the Light Division in the Peninsular War, often quoted, cover most points relating to inequalities of roads.

In any case, all depends on the officers On arriving in camp the temptation is great to stretch one's length on the ground and to stay there until the meal is prepared If, in place of doing so, Captain and subalterns will go among the men (and if the Colonel will note that they do) and direct the non-commissioned officers in looking after their squads to examine their foot gear and sore feet, the work, while it may be excessively monotonous day after day, will pay well for itself. Many men on arriving in camp prefer to lie about, dirty and travel-stained, and will not wash unless required to do so Sudden, absolute rest after fatigue, stiffens the joints and relaxes the system unduly. it is much better to move about and obtain the rest by degrees. Men should be compelled, after removing accoutrements, to take off their blouses, beat out the dust and place them where they will be aired and the perspiration be dried. then to loosen trousers and adjust their underclothing comfortably stockings should be changed, shoes greased while on, and feet, together with hands, face and neck, washed If the feet are tender or sore, hot water is much better for them than cold. Supper will also be more wholesome than if eaten immediately after prolonged exertion Men will soon observe this routine by preference and will need little supervision.

From this care and work will result willing, active, well trained, well seasoned, loyal soldiers, who, when called on for forced efforts—as they sometimes must be,—will respond cheerfully, and they will perform incredible feats without strewing the roads and fields with a string of fagged out, grumbling and insubordinate men.*

If the head of a column be attacked the most skillful tactics will be of no avail if the troops can not be brought up in good condition and the ammunition in sufficient supply.

An old maxim is to march by as many roads as possible provided the intervals are not too great to allow of easy communication and reciprocal support· but, as a rule, when near the enemy one is much limited in this respect. As a matter of fact, the several roads running in the same direction and the proper distance apart, are, in practice, not to be found. With large armies. it will seldom be possible to march less than a corps on one road. In May, 1864, Sheridan marched on the James River in a single column 13 miles long "for," he said, "I preferred this to the combinations arising from seperate roads, combinations rarely working as expected, and generally failing, unless subordinate officers are prompt and generally understand the situation."

The worst obstacle to a march is a timid or overcautious commander who allows a small retarding force in his front to stand in his way to induce him to halt and deploy. The commander must decide promptly whether or not the force can offer serious opposition and he must not be misled by noise and demonstrations. He should be able to judge from the reports of his cavalry whether there is any possibility or probability of the force in his front being considerable if he judge that it is not, the advance guard should be ordered to sweep it away and to keep it on the run. This was done by General Canby in his advance against Mobile when the enemy wished to gain time to perfect and reinforce his defences.

The great bugbear in marches is the weight which the soldier is expected to carry The question is a vexed one in all armies and admits of no solution because the average man is not strong enough to carry all that he needs in the field without being fatally encumbered Most soldiers solve it for themselves by sooner or later throwing away the knapsack, usually when going into action for the first or second time. German troops are now required to pile their knapsacks before battle it is said, they can be collected

* See note at the end of chapter

after a victory, while in case of defeat they would be discarded in any case. This is possible and will work well at maneuvres in war, no regiment knows, as a rule, at what moment it may be suddenly ordered forward under fire or whether the order will come or not. In the first case there will be only time enough for each man to discard his pack where he stands, while in case of uncertainty no one will know the right moment to pile knapsacks. In both cases the regiment will usually be far away from the spot after a battle. Men cling longest to great coat and blanket, seldom or never discarding the last. Unencumbered men can easily march one third farther than others.

It is difficult to discuss foot-gear temperately when men are permitted to buy and wear any kind of shoe they please. In theory they are supposed to select good shoes of a size which will fit; in practice they are judges neither of workmanship nor quality, are imposed on by cheap dealers or select fashionable shapes without regard to comfort. A shoe with square toe, double extension-sole, bellows-tongue, of grain leather, lacing well above the ankle and purchased of a first-class dealer at his own price will do much towards preventing straggling and will be very inexpensive in the end.* Shoes should be amply large but not loose. Stockings of pure wool are much the best to march in without regard to the season of the year; they are, however, expensive and cannot be kept from shrinking

Tentage, excepting to a limited extent, cannot be carried without extravagant allowance of wagons, yet some sort of shelter is desirable in most climates. In the South and Southwest, during the War of Secession few troops had tents, but the climate was mild. They suffered much, however, from cold at night and especially from prolonged rains. This suffering was largely temporary physical discomfort and did not affect their health unfavorably, colds and the like were unknown. In very cold weather tents without stoves are hardly an alleviation and men hug the camp fires outside. For a prolonged campaign with reduced transportation the choice must be between shelter tents, which add to the weight carried by the men, and bivouac. For eight months in the year and with plenty of fuel the latter can oftenbe made satisfactory and there will be an occasional apple tree or fence corner in the way of luxury

The fact is that on a long campaign no one can be comfortable excepting the higher and older officers, (as it is right they should)

---

*Shoes   w   a   ly ma k in any style and to fit any foot In case of war a Captain of foot troops can obtain a supply of shoes—if need be on his personal credit—for his command in a few days

unless the weather is fine· bad days must be met with youth and a philosophical frame of mind.

Note.—American, like English troops, do their duty soberly: they lack, in addition, the stimulus of traditions, brilliant uniforms and military song and story which relieve monotony and hardships in European battalions. In the Civil War, regimental bands, soon decimated, disappeared or were consolidated at distant Headquarters· tents and transportation were reduced to a minimum, and regular mails were possible only in the short intervals between campaigns. The day's march was often through a barren, nearly always through a thinly populated and deserted region, lacking the picturesque surroundings of people and villages, of hills and vineyards, which freshen the spirits of troops on the fertile plains of Europe. The one thing that could have been done for them was to supervise their marching. Often no word of of the length of the morrow's march reached the troops and men might husband their strength and available food and water or not as they saw fit,—and at the end of a reasonable number of miles undergo the most harrassing of all experiences of looking every few minutes for the sight of camp which would not come, perhaps for hours and until long after dark. Late at night, for, as a rule it was late when the last troops came in—a message would be sent to divisions, probably by a staff officer, naming the hour for march the next day. The same message was rapidly transmitted by mounted troopers to subdivisions—and this was all. Reveille was sounded about the same time everywhere and often troops got under arms and in ranks only to lie about until it was time to take the road. This seemed to depend largely on the subordinates down to regimental and even company commanders. If one of these, or a brigade commander, knowing that his command could not move until an indefinite time later, waited until what he himself took the responsibility of considering the last moment, it was an even chance that his men stood under arms an hour or more, previous to marching, either through excess of caution on his part or because of frequent halts of the column due to improper marching at its head or to obstacles on the road *which should have been discovered and removed the preceeding day* . The only orders insisted on during the march were to keep well closed up, to comply with which meant usually the most tiresome and wearing changes of gait from a run to a "mark time." Hourly rests, if ordered at all, were consumed in closing up, the tailing out being in most cases excessive, due to obstacles in the nature of defiles ahead. Word of these obstacles was rarely sent to the rear while they were being made passable or were being removed, so that troops at a sudden halt would waste opportunities for rest in waiting for the usual onward movement. Prolonged noon-day halts on account of heat or for food were exceptions, and the men often munched hardtack and whatever else they had while en route. Some time in the afternoon camp would be anxiously looked for, often hours in advance In any event the rearmost troops seldom reached it until after dark, the difficulties and fatigues of the road increasing many fold after sunset. Perhaps at 8 or 9 o'clock or later the reflected light of innumerable camp fires on the sky would indicate, unmistakably, "camp ahead." This meant inevitably a rather prolonged ⟨illegible⟩ filed off the road) and then a succession of ⟨illegible⟩ as the successive regiments were shown their ⟨illegible⟩

stacked many were content to throw themselves on the ground and sleep others would erect, anywhere, the bits of shelter tents to which they had clung: in all cases fires were started and coffee made, but rarely without a laborious search for wood and water, blinded by the many fires, knowing only the general direction, stumbling over sleeping troops lying in all directions and followed by their imprecations; and traversing the inequalities of unknown ground, stumps, logs, underbrush and morass in the dark or worse than dark, of the fire-light.

The picture is not overdrawn.

VII.

The concentration and strategic deployment of the German forces in 1870, profoundly planned and skillfully executed, placed France at the mercy of her antagonist, in advance even of the first collision, if the view which has been taken of modern strategy in these notes is correct. Modified by conditions which will differ in degree but not in kind, and by the size of the armies which will be employed, these operations must long serve as a model. Their study will show, it is believed:

1st. That the strategic plan must be made in advance and be ready when war is declared, because its execution depends on promptness of mobilization and concentration.

2nd. That its most vital problem will be the selection of a zone of concentration.

3rd. That it can lead only up to the first battles. The situation resulting from these will impose the necessity of adopting new plans from day to day, it may be from hour to hour.

4th. That "mistakes in the original massing of the armies can hardly be retrieved in the whole course of a campaign." "It is not impossible that a campaign unfortunately begun may suddenly, by a single victory, take a favorable course, but it is in the highest degree improbable." "The better strategical position of one side proclaims at once definitely its tactical superiority."*

The order for mobilization issued July 15th on the 23rd transport by rail to the frontier commenced: on the 30th the three armies occupied the line of the Rhine from Coblenz to Carlsruhe.

On July 30th the simple order which follows, initiated movements which resulted in the subjugation of France and in the destruction or capture of her armies.

"JULY 30, 9 o'clock P. M.

"His Majesty considers it expedient that as the Third Army is reinforced by the Baden and Würtemberg divisions, it should advance toward the south by the left bank of the Rhine to seek and attack the enemy. In this way the construction of bridges to

---
* von der Goltz

the south of Lauterburg will be prevented, and the whole of South Germany protected in the most effective manner."
(Signed) "VON MOLTKE."*

Moltke's plan. The plan was, simply, to unite the three armies on the northern frontier of France, between Luxemburg (the Moselle) and the Rhine where that river forms with the northern frontier nearly a right angle. In selecting this theatre of operations, therefore, he not only declined to utilize the Rhine as a line of defense but he left that portion of the German frontier open to the enemy Knowing, however, that the concentration would be accomplished before the French would advance in force he felt sure that the German advance towards the Moselle would "protect the whole of South Germany in the most effective manner."

This admirably conceived and masterly plan is characterized by simplicity and directness: it may even seem that its adoption should have been obvious now that its brilliant results are known and may be easily traced back to it. Any plan, however, which involved leaving, at the outset, the South German frontier open and unguarded, requiring the actual withdrawal from there of its natural protectors, the South German contingent, called for implicit confidence in the chief of the general staff together with courage and convictions on his part, of a high order.

The zone of concentration which was selected is divided in two by a range of mountains of considerable length; on the one side, the Rhine valley, on the other, the Palatinate. The latter was the real base of operations against the Moselle, with much the largest army of the three in the center closely connected with the First Army on its right and covered there by the neutral frontier of Luxemberg while in the Rhine valley, with the passes over the Vosges mountains, were assembled the troops, the Third Army, which on account of restricted space could not be deployed in the Palatinate and which, in any event, were required to cover the right flank.

Moltke assumed in his original, and, in a certain sense, provisional plan, that the German armies would be mobilized and concentrated on the frontier in fourteen days that the French

---
* The three armies were composed, as is well known, as follows
First Army (Steinmetz) I, VII, VIII, Corps 94,000
Second Army (Frederick Charles) II, III, IV, IX, XII, Guard Corps 228,000
Third Army (Crown Prince) V, VI, XI, I Bav II Bav , Baden Division, Würtemburg Division 195,000
The totals which represent "paper strength," are given at nearest round numbers in the fourth place, and ?' may be deducted The I, II and VI Corps did not join their respective armies until some time in August.

would take longer than this but that, in any event, their concentration would not begin until mobilization was completed. it therefore contemplated placing the Second and Third Armies on the frontier at once; but to provide against the possible violation of the neutrality of Luxemberg by the French the First Army was to assemble to the right and well to the rear of the second. This plan plainly designates the Second Army as the main body. which the First Army could readily reinforce, while the Third might, according to circumstances, be called on to remain on the defensive, to operate southward along the Rhine or, finally, to take the offensive and advance into France.

The German concentration was to take place, and did take place, principally by rail and it is interesting to note how skillfully the existing railroad lines were utilized in first bringing up troops where they were most needed and afterwards distributing the others according to the requirements of the situation as it developed.

Nine lines, in all, were used,—four of these, the three South German lines and the line from Münster being short and expected to transport rather less than one corps each. The VIII Corps, the Baden and Württemberg Divisions and the II Bavarian Corps could reach their destination in time, by marching. There were therefore five railroads available to transport the rest of the troops, nine corps, shortly increased to twelve. About two corps. therefore, fell to each road. Most of the railroads terminated at the Rhine, along which river most of the troops would be detrained. Only two lines extended beyond the river to the French frontier.

Four lines terminated in the zone of concentration of the Third Army, and this zone could be promptly occupied by the South German contingent by marching. It would be occupied then by a large force, before the advance troops of the first and second armies had begun to arrive elsewhere, consisting mainly of a contingent which the French, by promptly crossing the river, might otherwise endeavor to cut off and defeat separately.

Moltke's assumption that the French would first complete their mobilization and then concentrate was wrong. They assembled, instead, considerable forces along the eastern and northeastern frontier and these might easily combine and take the initiative by advancing into Germany. An advance by crossing the upper Rhine seemed improbable for obvious reasons and was however provided against by the position of German troops especially of those of the Third Army, while an advance into the Palatinate would be met by the main force, which was then being concentrated in proper shape and advancing with caution in view of this contingency.

French inactivity and the certainty that the neutral territory of Luxemberg would not be violated, speedily cleared the situation: and the frontier was finally occupied, in general, as follows.

The First Army on the line of the Saar from Merzig to Saarlouis, joining immediately on its left with the Second Army, which extended from Saarlouis beyond Sarreguemines Both together, therefore, formed a single group of about 200,000 men (not including the corps in reserve) occupying a front of about thirty miles, about 6,500 men to the mile. At this time this group was about twice as strong as the Third Army: its organization in two "armies," while perhaps no longer called for, was retained. The The Third Army, then about 130,000 strong was concentrated between Laudan and Carlsruhe on a front of about twenty miles, also with about 6,500 men to the mile. It was divided unequally in two by the Rhine, but ample facilities for crossing were provided 6,500 men to the mile of front is about 3½ men to the yard or about one-half the number with which the Germans attacked in the first battles; and about one-half the number with which the Federals defended the position at Gettysburg.

Between Sarregemines and Laudan is the mountainous region, about fifty miles wide which the Germans occupied by a small corps of observation. Its main highway into France was commanded by the French fortress of Bitche.

It is clear from the geographical character of this region that the two groups of armies were intended to operate separately as no junction would be possible, unless it were by an advance into France or by a retreat into Germany. The reserve corps, however, which had been concentrated in rear on the Rhine were so placed as to be able to reinforce either group or both, at pleasure

The strategic deployment and march to the frontier of the Second Army.—The zone of concentration of the Second Army was the Rhine between Bingen and Mannheim.

On July 25th the advance troops were detraining on this line. Instead, however, of being pushed forward at once they were held to await the completion of the large units near the stations, because it was now known that the French occupied the frontier in considerable force and might make a forward movement

By July 30th it was believed that no offensive movement on the part of the French need be looked for. The army was therefore ordered to the left bank of the river to occupy the strong defensive position on the eastern slope of the mountains, Alsenz, Grünstadt, Gölheim.

On July 31st the III and IV Corps occupied this line, while the IX and XII received orders to push forward to it as soon as possible.

The 5th and 6th cavalry divisions had been sent forward to the frontier to explore. On the 31st they formed three columns, holding the two highroads from Mayence and Mannheim to Sarrebrück, while a regiment established connection between the Second and Third Armies at Pirmasens. The front of exploration was about 45 miles.

Up to August 3rd the forward movement of the army was conducted with great caution because, in the first place an offensive movement on the part of the French was still deemed possible, and also because the corps were still being reinforced and completed by the last troops from the detraining stations. Two advance detraining stations had, in the mean time, been established at Baumholder and Kaiserslantern. Communication with the First Army had been established at Tholey.

In case of an offensive movement the line of the Lauter, between Offenbach and Kaiserslantern was to be occupied (August 2nd, 3rd), presumably with the III Corps on the right, the IV Corps on the left, the IX Corps in the center, with the X Corps, XII Corps, and the Guard Corps within call. Otherwise the III and IV Corps were to advance a short day's march and await the closing up of all the corps to within half a day's march. This latter movement was inaugurated so that August 3rd, 4th, the army was in two lines as follows:

In the first line the III and IV Corps, their advance troops at Konken and Bruchmühlbach, on a front of about 15 miles.

In the second line the Guard Corps was at Kaiserslantern, the IX, XII and X Corps advancing from Grünstadt, Alzey and Fürfeld, respectively.

The exploring cavalry was 25 miles in advance, quite close to the frontier and covering a front of about 20 miles.

In these positions the corps held the wooded and hilly country on the western slope of the Hardt, on a narrow front, in great depth and ready at any time to take up a strong defensive position. Its next marches would result in the deployment of the army beyond the wooded defiles, the deployment being covered on the right by the First Army

This deployment was originally intended to take place August 7th. It was known that the French had attacked Sarrebrück and made demonstrations towards Völkingen and Saareguemines, which might or might not indicate a general offensive movement on their part; moreover the Third Army was to take the offensive the next day (4th), and the result of this movement was to be awaited If victorious, the First and Second armies would at once advance to the Sarre, while the forward movement of the Third army would cover their left flank

But already on the 4th it became known that the Second Army could deploy from its defiles without fear of attack and preliminary orders for the march were given.

This knowledge was obtained from the reports of the cavalry and especially from those of the 6th cavalry division, which were promptly transmitted to Headquarters. On receiving information of the combat of August 2nd at Sarrebrück, the commanding officer of this division, not content with any explanation of the French movement, no matter how plausible, promptly despatched a squadron on each of four principal roads leading from the vicinity of Ottweiler to the frontier with orders to keep in contact with the French forces wherever found. These squadrons reached the frontier, attacked patrols, took prisoners and discovered that the enemy's columns were everywhere retiring. Following these, the brigade on the extreme left, at Zweibrücken, sent forward five detachments, each of several squadrons, which pushed on, ten miles beyond the frontier and viewed the camps at Rohrbach and Bitche On the right the cavalry penetrated to the vicinity of Forbach, five miles *in rear* of the formost French positions

In consequence of the information received directly, or indirectly (through General Headquarters) from the cavalry, and for other reasons which will be mentioned further on, the Second Army advanced into the open region of the Sarre and on the evening of the 5th held the following positions on four roads, Neunkirchen—Sarrebruck, Homburg—St. Ingbert, Homburg—Sarreguemines, Einöd—Rohrbach, leading from the Neunkirchen—Zweibrücken line to the frontier: III Corps, Neunkirchen,—advance guard at Sulzbach, 6 miles in front; X Corps, probably on or near the road Neunkirchen—Homburg, about half way between these places, advance guard 8 miles off at St. Ingbert, Guard Corps on the line Homburg—Einod, IV Corps near

Zweibrücken, little more than one mile from the frontier, its advance guard on the line, IX Corps in rear at Waldmohr, and the XII Corps advancing from Bruchmühlbach.

The front of march was now that of a line of battle which the six corps deployed would occupy with about seven men per yard of front, while the furthest troops were less than a day's march in rear

The formation may be considered to be in three echelons, each of two corps

The frontier was to be crossed by the heads of all the columns at the same time. As is well known, this plan was frustrated by the advance of part of the VII Corps of the First Army.

Comments. The foregoing sketch of the strategic deployment of the Second Army and the march to the frontier from its zone of concentration on the Rhine, is a general outline only, and is not exact The salient features of the movement as it was planned, ordered and, to a great extent, executed, are given, unencumbered by non-essential details which would obscure the narrative while adding to its accuracy. Some of these details follow

On July 28th, only two corps, the III and IV, had finished detraining at Bingen and Mannheim, respectively. As, at this time, the Third Army had attained sufficient strength to hold its own, these two corps were no longer needed on the Rhine and it was convenient if not necessary for them to vacate cantonments for troops to arrive. They were therefore ordered forward to the Alsenz line, on the 29th, which line they would reach on the 31st. The IX and XII Corps were not concentrated near Mayence until August 2nd, while the X and Guard Corps did not finish detraining until the 5th, though it is true that their detraining stations had been advanced to the line Kaiserslautern—Baumholder. It would seem, therefore that the strict separation between concentration, strategic deployment, and attack of the frontier, which the Germans inculcate, was not observed and could not be; for the rapid developing of the situation demanded that these operations be carried on, nolens volens, simultaneously.

When the Second Army was ordered to occupy the Alsenz line, only two corps, the III and IV, were ready to march * They would reach the new position on the 31st, and it was evidently the intention that they should hold it, or, at most, advance slowly, until some of the corps in rear could advance to supporting

---

* The IV Corps complete the III was not completed until August

distance. As a matter of fact the two corps continued to march towards the line of the Lauter—and this, again, it would seem, because the regular sequence of events had been disturbed and it was already necessary to meet the new. In anticipation of the march of the Second, the First Army was assembling in the neighborhood of Wadern, therefore well in advance of the general line: with the Second Army stationary the first would be isolated not only by its position and distance from the Second but because of the nature of the country which separated them. Then, again, it had become necessary to utilize the railroads beyond the original zone of concentration and to advance the detraining stations for two corps: to cover these an advance was imperative. Finally, the 5th and 6th cavalry divisions had been ordered to the frontier line and it was deemed advisable to support them by a division from each of the two corps, beyond the defiles of the Hardt.

It is worthy of note that the 5th and 5th cavalry divisions were not ordered to the front until July 30th, and that up to that date no exploration of the frontier by cavalry had been organized. This was undoubtedly due to the slowness with which the mounted troops were entrained, to difficulties of furnishing their transportation and to the fact that they were not, as a rule, forwarded until a large proportion of infantry had already reached the zone of concentration. These obstacles will exist in future and it will be necessary hereafter to station permanently large bodies of cavalry near those frontier regions in which war may be looked for, to protect the concentration, to disturb or prevent that of the enemy and to keep in touch with his columns. As the 5th and 6th divisions could not reach the frontier line until the 3rd or 4th, it is clear that their presence and advance was not intended to protect and cover the concentration of the Second Army, because that concentration had then been accomplished, i. e., if any particular date may be accepted as marking its termination. The date usually given in narratives of the war is the 29th or 30th of July, but the last effectives did not join the Third Army until August 3rd, the day before its first action, and did not join the Second Army until the 5th, on the eve of Spicheren, (indeed, one battery was detrained on the field during the progress of the battle), while long after these dates the transport to the frontier of parts of the I, II and VI Corps was still going on.

It must not be forgotten, however, that, though it was defective in more than minor details, *the concentration was not begun until mobilization was finished* and no matter what proportion of its effective force or what part of its equipment this or that corps might lack, it stood ready somewhere, complete in everything, to be forwarded at the first favorable opportunity. This was the radical distinction between French and German methods at that time.

The advantages attending rapid and systematic concentration were so conspicuous in this war that since then many have been satisfied to trace to them alone, the brilliant results which followed. It is quite certain that, in future, plans of mobilization, transport and assemblement will be perfected and tested in peace with the greatest diligence and that the first effort in war will be to interfere with and, if possible, upset the concentration of an adversary In 1870, the concentration of the German armies was undisturbed, in spite of which fact it was necessary to modify original plans at more or less critical moments and it is easy to understand how, at one time, an enterprising enemy could have played havoc with them. Hereafter, liberty to concentrate with comparative leisure must be purchased in battles which will take place between masses—for the most part, mounted troops—far in advance of the zone and ready in position at the outbreak of war. Every effort will be made to transfer the theatre of this preliminary warfare to the adversary's territory.

The First Army. The line of the Sarre between Merzig and Sarrelouis was assigned originally to be occupied by the First Army. At that time this consisted of the VII and VIII Corps only and on July 31st the VII stood concentrated at Trèves. The VIII, on that day, had two or three regiments on the frontier line and other troops were en route, so that the corps was making a movement forward by various roads, all leading in the direction of Sarrebrück, in a depth of about 60 miles. In the mean time orders from General Headquarters required the First Army to occupy the line, from Wadern east, by August 3rd. This was a precautionary order to prevent the First Army from advancing at a rate which must result in isolating its operations, but it soon transpired that the cantonments of its foremost troops already overlapped those of the Second Army. It therefore received orders to incline to the right "But its chief, fearing to be deprived of the honor of giving the first blows, had cleared the ground by pushing his troops upon the frontier. In consequence, one of his corps, the VII, took measures to move its advance-guard upon Sarrebruck. This move ren..... t the battle of Spicheren.

The Third Army. This army was intended to act independently, only if opposed by a considerable French force If unopposed or if confronted by a containing force it was to brush this aside and by the direction of its march unite with the advancing Second Army, west of the Vosges. It was possible to increase its effective by one or all of three corps, then in rear, or to reduce it by one or two corps by withdrawing these to join the troops on the Sarre. At the end of July, the distribution of the French army was pretty accurately known at German General Headquarters, and it was thought best—as it was certainly most convenient—to finally add one additional corps to each of the three armies. The right wing and center were then so strong that it would be exceedingly difficult to employ the entire force at the same time, and for this reason, if for no other, the effective strength of the Third Army was not reduced, but increased by the VI Corps. Under the reasonable supposition that the French would act with ordinary prudence and perhaps with much skill, the plan at that time was an advance by all three armies to confront the enemy with an overwhelming force beyond the Sarre. With this in view, the Third Army, which had the longest and most difficult route, was ordered to advance first. It was expected to unite with the center, in the neighborhood of Sarreguemines about August 9th. In any case the direction of its march would threaten the right of the French and it might be conducted so as to threaten their rear.

However interesting, it is idle to discuss now what the French should have done or even what, under the circumstances, they might have done; for these considerations are not relevant to the lesson which it is sought to inculcate. The lesson is this That a good general plan, simple in its features and unhampered by profound combinations, executed with decision, but with the caution which does not underrate an adversary, is the best part of strategy.

The conception of such a plan requires professional skill and experience of the highest order, and it must be laboriously tested with an exact knowledge of details and minutiae. Its execution requires the best organization, discipline and morale, an infinite amount of painstaking, monotonous work during peace, and persistent drill, especially in that higher sense which ensures co-operation of the three arms of the service combined

"These conditions can not be created by the genius of a general-in chief, but rather by the prudence of governments, and by the sacrifices that a people is willing to make. Those people who, distracted by preoccupations of another kind, neglect them during peace," must be content to rely—as a rule in vain—on whatever brilliant tours de force their leaders may be able to devise.

Some of the comments which the German operations have called forth, however irrelevant to the main point at issue, will help to a better understanding.

"In 1870 a certain independence in the operations of the First and Second Armies on the one hand, and of the Third Army on the other is recognizable. While the Crown Prince was passing the Vosges his communications with the other leaders could only have been by the telegraph lines in his rear; and he continued to move on a distinct line towards Chalons, while they advanced on Metz. It might therefore at first seem that the Germans were operating by a double line. But their base—namely the Rhine to Germersheim—was common and continuous and their main lines of advance were never more than from thirty to forty miles apart, so that their flanking troops and outposts must generally have been nearly within a march of each other." "With the disparity of force existing in this campaign, it must be doubtful whether the French, if in other respects more equal to their adversaries than they proved to be, could have successfully maintained a forward position. But had they been so well informed as they should have been of the intentions and movements of the enemy up to the 6th, August, they might have contested the frontier line with very different results, even if at last compelled to retire by superior numbers." "Their course, if they were resolved to defend the frontier, seems clear. Nothing but superior concentration, in conjunction with a proper use of the topographical advantages for defence, could avail against numbers so disproportionate. A retarding force on one side of the theatre would have gained time for the action of an army capable of striking a blow on the other. Two circumstances pointed to the Crown Prince's line of advance as that on which the French retarding force should be placed. 1st, it lay through the most difficult and defensible country, 2nd, the retreat might be conducted for some time without laying bare the communications of the co-operating army on the other line." "Looking at the situation on the 6th, it seems impossible to doubt that their advance might have been roughly checked, and that the French, if compelled by superior numbers to fall back would have retired with a very different aspect on the prepared line of the Moselle."*

---
* Hamley

"Several writers have held that the First Army should have been attacked in force while taking up the Wadern line. If attacked then, they claim, it would have been obliged to fight under unfavorable circumstances or have retreated. The claim is undoubtedly quite true, though it is not clear just what the French could have accomplished after forcing the retreat There seems to have been friction in this case, in carrying out the German plan, either by a neglect at General Headquarters to keep the First Army in touch with the Second, or because it was difficult to keep under control the commander-in-chief of the First Army without trespassing at the same time on his prerogative as an independent commander. The German official account makes the following good natured explanation:

"The First Army could avoid an attack from superior forces in the mountainous ground, which was extremely favorable for the purpose." * * * "It was unmistakable that there was a considerable difference in the opinions and in the first intentions prevailing at the Royal Head-Quarters and at the Head-Quarters of the First Army respectively." "The First Army was assembled before either of the other two. It was nearest to the enemy and formed an offensive flank for the Second Army, at all events until the latter arrived on the same line with it. General v Steinmetz therefore endeavored from the commencement to draw the enemy's forces upon himself just as he had done with success at the beginning of the campaign of 1866 " "When the position at Tholey was subsequently taken up in virtue of superior orders, and troops of the Second Army already extended westward beyond the quarters of the First Army, General v. Steinmetz had cause for apprehension that any longer delay on his part might throw him completely into second line in the event of the corps of Prince Frederick Charles reaching the frontier before him " "Up to this time General v. Steinmetz had only received delaying or hampering instructions from the Royal Head-Quarters. He therefore wished to have more comprehensive directions extending over a longer period, during which he could preserve the desired freedom for his own resolutions· On the other hand, the opinion was held at the Royal Head-Quarters that neither the Second, much less the weaker First Army, should be exposed singly to a collision with the French main force." * * * "It consequently appeared essential to halt it for a time at Tholey."

"It was expected at the Royal Head-Quarters that the French army would be found, if not earlier, at any rate in position behind the Moselle with its flanks resting on Thionville and Metz

In this event the First Army was to engage the enemy in front, while the Second was to attack him directly in flank, from the southward. During the wheel of one-eighth of a circle to the right, which this operation rendered necessary, the First Army, having the shortest line to traverse, formed the pivot; it ought to leave the roads by which the right wing of the Second Army marched, perfectly free."

"As every day might usher in some great decisive result, the Royal Head-Quarters thought that it could not give any directions extending beyond the immediate events. It was rather, considered permissible and necessary on this and subsequent critical occasions, to control the movements of the large units by definite orders from the Royal Head-Quarters, however much that arrangement might provisionally limit the independence of the commanders of armies."

VIII.

OBJECTIVES —The selection of the theatre of operations to be occupied, requires previous knowledge of the nature and extent of whatever obstacles may be utilized or must be overcome, together with a just estimate of their relative military importance.

The possession, destruction or removal of one or more of them will augment an army's power for action. These are then called "Strategic Points," and they become "Objective Points" or "Objectives."

The side which is best prepared and first ready will be able to select the theatre of operations If the selection is wise, the adversary will have no choice other than direct opposition For this reason and *because it is the soverign obstacle the enemy's army should always be the first objective.*

The surest, shortest, most economical and most effective way to defeat an enemy is to seek and attack his army.

However elementary and evident this conclusion may seem, it has time and again been ignored. Wars abound from their beginning in apparent opportunities to keep one's cake and eat it— "to make omelets without breaking eggs"—to cripple an enemy and bring him to terms by indirect methods, which are very promising and very enticing. It requires good judgment together with firmness and strength of purpose to disregard them, and to resist pressure due to solicitude or local interests and to the inevitable schemes of amateurs in the forum and press.

In the War of Secession, it is no doubt true that "the magnitude of the task which the North proposed to itself—the conquest of such a vast territory, defended by such an able, resolute, and gallant population—was not fully seen at the beginning " It is also true that a flood of political questions seemed to demand immediate attention and that the situation was abnormally involved by them. But as early as 1861, General McClellan, in his report, could put the military aspect very clearly as follows.

"The object of the present war differs from those in which nations are usually engaged mainly in this, that the purpose of ordinary war is to conquer a peace and make a treaty on advantageous terms In this contest it has become necessary to crush a population sufficiently warlike to constitute a nation. We have not only to defeat their armed and organized forces in the field, but to display such an overwhelming strength as will convince all our antagonists, especially those of the governing, aristocratic class, of the utter impossibility of resistance." "The rebels have chosen Virginia as their battle-field, and it seems proper for us to make the first great struggle there."

Now the best way "to display overwhelming strength" after defeating armed and organized forces in the field was to follow them up and defeat them again and as often as necessary, and, so far, General McClellan was correct. But like everyone else he was unable to banish from his mind the idea that the enemy must be crippled elsewhere in his vast territory, in some of the many sections where independent operations seemed to promise valuable results. The Mississippi must be opened, Missouri and West Virginia secured, East Tennessee occupied, and he advocates "the employment of a strong naval force, to protect the movement of a fleet of transports intended to convey a considerable body of troops from point to point of the enemy's sea-coast, thus either creating diversions and rendering it necessary for them to detach largely from their main body in order to protect such of their cities as may be threatened, or else landing and forming establishments on their coast at any favorable places that opportunity might offer. This naval force should also co-operate with the main army in its efforts to seize the important seaboard towns of the rebels."

That no attempt to carry out this plan was ever made is well known, but for three years afterwards a military policy was pursued by the North, beside which it seems simple and direct. "For three years there was presented the lamentable spectacle of three or four independent armies, acting on various lines of operations, and working not only with no unity of purpose, but frequently at cross-purpose," while "in Virginia, the Army of the Potomac had not only to combat the main army of the South, but an army that by means of the interior lines held by the Confederates, might be continually strengthened from the forces in the western zone, unless these should be under such constant pressure as to prevent their diminution "*

In addition to the numerous grand operations which were undertaken throughout the South and Southwest every year, either in continuation of others. to retrieve failure, or planned anew, the number of inferior expeditions runs up into the hundreds. These were frequently undertaken by, and at the request of some sub-

*Swinton.

ordinates, had no well defined objects other than "to injure the enemy," while, as often as not they resulted disastrously and goaded an already exasperated people to desperation. Grand operations which aimed at penetrating and holding whole sections of country at well defined strategic points, seemed to, and no doubt did, require diversions on the part of troops distributed so widely, that combinations offered themselves freely

In February, 1864, General Sherman marched from the Mississippi River to Meridian, Mississippi, across the whole state, with an army of 20,000 men, to destroy the Mobile and Ohio Railroad General W. S. Smith was to co-operate with 10,000 cavalry by attacking Forrest further north. Smith failed to co-operate and General Sherman after destroying many miles of railroad returned to Vicksburg and Memphis. Of this expedition which occupied 30,000 of the finest troops for a month. General Sherman says in his report: "My object was to break up the enemy's railroads at and about Meridian, and to do the enemy as much damage as possible in the month of February, and to be prepared by the first of March to assist General Banks in a similar dash* at the Red River country, especially Shreveport, the whole to result in widening our domain along the Mississippi River, and thereby set the troops hitherto necessary to guard the river, free for other military purposes." After recapitulating the results of the expedition, General Sherman says· "I attach little importance to these matters, but the great result attained is the hardihood and confidence imparted to the command, which is now better fitted for war. Animals and men returned to Vicksburg after marching from 360 to 450 miles in the space of the shortest month in the year, in better health and condition than when we started."

This expedition is, in kind, only one of a great number imposed on commanders nearly everywhere outside of Virginia; penalties which had to be paid to keep the imaginary gains of a wasteful and vicious military policy. Sherman, who was a great soldier, understood this well. Only a few weeks later he could say—as he afterwards did say—that his army at Chattanooga was Grant's "right" in other words that every successful step in his operations would strike, however indirectly, at the true objective, the main force of the enemy in front of Richmond.

To a certain extent General Grant himself was obliged to accept the situation as he found it Diffusion had obtained certain

---

* This "similar dash" was the well known disastrous Red River Expedition, under Banks The assistance given by General Sherman (A J Smith's Corps) averted total defeat, if not

results, each in itself of value, which it was not desirable to waste. When General Sherman started on his march to the sea, he arranged that 15,000 men under General A J. Smith (the same force which had averted ruin on the Red River) *then engaged in repelling Price's maurading expedition in Missouri,* should be sent to General Thomas. Their co-operation in Missouri was, as it proved, not vital, and Thomas was informed that they would leave St. Louis about November 10th. As a matter of fact, Smith had to march across the whole state and did not arrive at St. Louis until the 24th. "Had he come at the proposed time it was General Thomas's intention to place him at Eastport, on the Tennessee River, so as to threaten Hood's flank and rear if the latter advanced. With such disposition the battle of Franklin and Nashville would have been relegated to the category of events which never come to pass. But when Smith reached St Louis, Hood was threatening Columbia; and it was an open question whether he would not reach Nashville before the reinforcements from Missouri." No reinforcement "was ever more anxiously awaited than this."

As in wider, so in narrower strategical movements, it seems to have been difficult to resist the temptation to employ troops— especially cavalry—in diversions or what not. "What fascinated the ingenious mind of the American general, was a raid, designed to burn bridges and tear up railroad tracks, to destroy supplies, capture trains, and the like. * * * What good was accomplished in this way has never been figured up. Stuart's raid around McClellan's lines in June, 1862, may have served a useful purpose in creating a feeling of insecurity in the Army of the Potomac; but the only tangible result of the repetition of the performance in August of the same year, was the capture of the overcoat of the Federal Commander, while, when for the third time the maneuvre was tried, in the Gettysburg campaign the next summer, the march of the Federal army westward actually prevented the Confederate cavalry from rejoining their main army and reporting the movements of the Federals. It was much the same in our experience. Hooker no sooner got a large and finely mounted and equipped body of cavalry together, than he sent them off, a fortnight before he commenced his own campaign, to destroy the enemy's communications and supplies, and to render their retreat, in the event of a Federal success in the impending struggle between the two armies, more disastrous than it otherwise could be The result of this far seeing move was to deprive the army of the Potomac of the information which would have prevented the great disaster of the campaign of Chancellorsville." * * * "The campaign of 1864 had hardly opened when Sheridan was allowed to go off, on his own suggestion and evidently against Meade's judgement, with nearly all the cavalry of the army, on a raid toward Richmond, and it was not until Grant had crossed the Pamunky that the cavalry rejoined the main body. Then, for a very few days, they remained with the army, and rendered excellent service, among other things, capturing and holding Cold Harbor. But when, a fortnight later, the army had got down to Petersburg, Sheridan was on another raid, and the opportunity which really existed during the 16th and 17th of June of taking Petersburg when its defenders numbered less than fifteen thousand men was unknown at headquarters, simply for lack of cavalry to make the needed reconnoisances." * * * "In spite of all the railroad ties that were torn up, and of all the barns that were burned, General Lee did not leave Petersburg and Richmond until the result of the battle of Five Forks rendered it impossible for him to remain in his lines.'

"It is almost inconceivable to us now, that General Lee should have sent Stuart, with less than two thousand cavalry, in October, 1862, just after the battle of Antietam, to ride through the towns and counties of central Pennsylvania, picking up horses, clothing, boots and shoes, a few prisoners, and what not, and running the most imminent risk of being captured with his whole command. What possible good could Stuart do to the Confederacy with his petty booty, which could not be compared for a moment with the exultation with which the news of his capture would have been received at the North, and the injury which it would have been to General Lee's army to have lost its great cavalry leader? So in the Gettysburg campaign—when Lee actually gave Stuart carte blanche to do as he liked—whether to keep between the Army of Northern Virginia and the Army of the Potomac, or to attempt to make the circuit of the latter army." * * * "At that stage in the war, it was out of the question that the Federal army should be 'rattled' by any such game as this. Both officers and men were too well seasoned to war to care very much where Stuart's four or five thousand men might be. The trains were well guarded; all Stuart succeeded in bagging were a hundred and twenty-five wagons and four or five hundred prisoners, but, as this was all he had to show in justification of his course, he brought them all in, notwithstanding the continual delays caused by such impediments. General Halleck was probably the only Federal officer at all worried by this eccentric movement of Stuart's, and he kept telegraphing Meade, who was in command of the Army of the Potomac, to take measures to capture Stuart's column, which might, so Halleck thought, do unknown damage somewhere. But Meade, intent on the great task before him, was not to be diverted by any side-show like this. 'My main point,' he cooly and dryly wrote to Halleck, 'being to find out and fight the enemy, I shall have to submit to the cavalry raids around me in some measure.' "*

Other objectives.—Text writers have distinguished and classified other objectives and have ransacked military history for instances when these have been an army's first aim. From this classification have resulted principal, secondary, geographical, decisive, contingent objectives and objectives of maneuvre. The consideration of these would be interesting but not valuable. Essentially, the enemy's main army is, first and last, the only objective; deviations from this rule have been either apparent only, or have been mistakes. Railroad centers, fortified places and the like, form no exception as long as their possession prevents reinforcement of the enemy, cuts off his retreat or facilitates the advance of the attack.

The enemy's capital has nearly always been a secondary, and sometimes a principal objective. The reasons, in general, for this, lie on the surface and are very human; but they are not always good military reasons. It is easy to trace the down-fall of Napoleon to Berlin, 1806, Madrid, 1808, and Moscow, 1812. On the other hand when the Allies pushed for the Capital in 1814, they had first worn Napoleon out; and the occupation of Paris, moreover, would lead, it was known, to his dethronement and to peace.

The capture of Richmond at any time during the War of Secession, with Lee's army practically intact, would not have shortened the war: indeed there were those in the South who repeatedly urged its abandonment as an element of weakness.

In 1866, the Prussians marched on Vienna, after Sadowa, because that was the direction of the Austrian retreat, and, for reasons which are now known, they never had the intention of entering the Capital under any circumstances. In 1870 they were not so wise. The march on Paris was undoubtedly demanded by public opinion at home, and stimulated by grim memories, in short, by motives which were 'very human' but in a military sense it was an expensive blunder. The monarchy had fallen,

---
* Ropes

the last regular soldier was in captivity or in Metz, and Germany held a third or more of the country as security for pecuniary and territorial indemnity. She preferred to take a course which roused the most formidable national opposition, prolonged the war for many months, permanently embittered a neighboring people and, at one time, placed her cause in peril

Strategic lines.—These have been conveniently divided into "bases of operations," "fronts of operations," "lines of operations," and "lines of communications:"

Bases of operations.—It has always been necessary, as it is necessary today, to have somewhere in rear of an army a portion of territory with which it keeps up communication and from which it is supplied. Formerly this was a comparatively contracted section in which stores of all kinds had been collected, workshops established, hospitals erected and depots organized for recruits. It was usually easily defensible and strongly fortified, from it the army obtained supplies and reinforcements, transferred to it the sick, wounded and unserviceable material, and counted on it as a line of defence or place of refuge in case of reverses. It was, in short, imperative, to collect the supplies of a country in advance and to focus them at some place convenient to the army, because communication between one part of the country and another was very slow, and because factories and workshops capable of turning out at short notice many things which an army needs, did not then exist, as they do now, in every other town.

Railroads have rendered compact, thoroughly organized bases like this no longer necessary. except, for the convenience of retaining the term it would be expedient to hold that bases of operations were out of date and absolete. For while it would not then be necessary to invent a new term, it is now necessary to select a new section of territory to which the old term may be applied.

The rather indefinite territory selected is, *"the frontier zones by which the armies communicate with their country"* and *"which to-day constitute true bases of operations."** This will not only include the zone of concentration but also that zone in advance of it in which the strategic deployment takes place.

This zone has some of the characteristics of the old bases of operations. It is selected in advance; it is, or should be at first, directly in rear of the line of advance, and it is strong by nature

---
* Derrécagaix

and perhaps by the protection of neutral frontiers or has "fortified places which guarantee possession of the railroads connecting the base with the country itself," while the returning sick and wounded there reach home and have the care and attention which they could not receive at the actual seat of war.

These bases of operations are, however, in no sense, bases of supply. The corps districts, the whole country, every town and hamlet, contribute whatever they can, and what they can furnish is accumulated by many kinds of roads and transport, at places on the main lines of railway. "At the end of July, 1870, the Germans had collected six weeks supplies for seven corps, at Cologne, Coblenz, Bingen, Mayence and Mannheim." * * * "All these places were either principal or branch-point stations on railroads leading to the Rhine. Forseeing the difficulties of providing for the troops during their transportation to the frontier, the commissary service had, in addition, accumulated six weeks supplies in each corps region. A portion of these was carried by the troops to the zone of concentration. And up to the day when the railroads were available for the transportation of provisions, the armies were fed from these supplies, those found at the cantonments, and especially those brought together in the cities of the Rhine. Even by making the most of the local resources, the German commissary department recognized the fact that the Rhenish provinces, notwithstanding their fruitfulness, would be able to furnish but two days provisions to the troops assembled in the zone of concentration. During the first days of August, when the German armies had become assured of the defensive attitude of the French, the dispositions made with reference to their supply-centres were modified."

From this "it is seen that the chief modifications in bases have been in the location of Magazines, depots, hospitals, &c. These are upon the principal railroads in rear of the base."

"France in 1870, had for its base of operations the Metz-Strasburg zone, but it was an offensive base, established in anticipation of events whose course was arrested by the first engagements. The mistake was made of establishing the first supplies upon this base, instead of placing them upon the railroads in rear. These supplies consequently fell into the hands of the enemy, when one of the points supporting the base was taken."*

Extent of bases of operations.—The direction of bases of operations has been already discussed. In extent they should permit convenient supply and the ability to concentrate or light-

---
* Derrécagaix

ing The latter means that the entire force must, if necessary, be so echeloned that it can unite in battle at 24 hours notice Beyond this, the longer the base which, in case of necessity, *can be occupied,* the better, because the line of communications can be changed at will and be at the same time covered In the War of Secession the Federals had the single but distinct advantage of being able to change their base at will without exposing the successive lines of communications. This was due both to the direction and intent of the dividing lines between the two adversaries.

Derrécagaix summs up these considerations as follows.

"1st. *Bases of operations have been transformed by the establishment of railroads;*"

"2nd. *The supplies formerly assembled upon the bases, will henceforth be established along the railroads charged with army transport service;*"

"3rd. *Bases of operations are frontier zones which connect the armies with their countries, and upon which they concentrate before the commencement of operations,*"

"4th. *The direction of the base, with regard to the enemy's lines of operations, increases in importance in proportion as the masses become more numerous and the first conflicts more imminent,*"

"5th. *An angular base is always the most advantageous;*"

"6th. *There should be a sufficient number of railroads running from the interior of the country to the base to assure the prompt concentration of the army*"

Fronts of operation.—This is a convenient term by which to designate the space occupied by the heads of columns of an army Some writers call this the "strategic front" and apply the expression "front of operations" to the space between two opposing armies. The former application is the better because it applies to a line the length of which the commander-in-chief must control and which must fulfil certain conditions.

The most important of these is that the front must be so limited that the army may be concentrated for battle in a day, or in other words, that no corps will have to make more than a day's march to enter the line of battle

This principle is so important and at the same time so simple that it would be gratuitous to assume that because it was often violated in the War of Secession, its importance was not perceived. As a matter of fact it is often very difficult to live up to it—often impossible in a theatre where there are few roads and where they are bad. In such cases any advance must be laborious and slow, preceeded and flanked by strong cavalry forces and the trains kept well in rear. The neglect of these precautions led to the failure of the expensive and well organized Red River Expedition in 1864. In his otherwise long and explicit report of the campaign the commanding general makes the following inadequate and scant explanation.

"The result of the position of the cavalry train and the loose order of march by the leading column of troops, on the 8th of April, before the battle of Sabine Cross Roads, has been stated. A commanding officer is, of course, responsible for all that occurs to his command, whatever may have been the cause. I do not shrink from that responsibility. But" * * * "it was supposed that the movement of a single column of 13,000 men, moving in advance on one road for a distance of less than 50 miles in such manner as to enable them to encounter the enemy if he offered resistance, might safely be intrusted to an officer" * * * "whose rank, except in one instance, was superior to that of any officer of the expedition or in the Department of the Gulf.'

In the summer of 1864 it was thought important to engage General Forrest, to disperse his forces and to destroy the Mobile and Ohio Railroad To do this 8.000 or 9,000 men of all arms were sent out from Memphis. This force was routed, or as its commander expresses it in his first, short report: "Our loss in killed and wounded is very heavy. We have lost most everything, including a number of wagons and artillery, and ammunition." In forwarding the detailed report, General Sherman says * * * "I do know that misfortunes may befall us all, and these are rendered more likely in wooded countries, with narrow roads and deep mud. He was dealing with a bold and daring foe, on fresh horses, familiar with the roads and by-paths, and perfectly unencumbered with trains. I consider a train of wagons reduces a command just one half, for it cannot move without covering its train."

The proceedings of the board which was convened to investigate and report on this disaster cover innumerable pages, but its verdict may be condensed into a single sentence. "The immediate cause of the defeat, was meeting the masses of the enemy with fractions."

This campaign, one of many, utterly uncalled for and wasteful in their inception was undoubtedly lost, primarily, by mismanagement. Still, there are many reasons—explanations if not excuses—why great skill, forethought and vigilance were required to meet the unencumbered, enterprising and embittered enemy on anything like equal terms. The roads, or more truthfully, the road, was of a kind which made it convenient if not obligatory on individuals, to travel on horseback. in effect it was simply a succession of defiles. While the invading force was compelled to operate under explicit orders, the "front of operations" was, as often as not, a swamp; and it had rained for eight successive days. The reports, which are very voluminous, illustrate many principals which have been insisted on in these notes and extracts from them are given, almost at random, as follows.

General Sturgis. "It became a serious question in my mind whether or not I should proceed any farther. The rain still fell in torrents. The artillery and wagons were literally mired down, and the starved and exhausted animals could with difficulty drag them along "

Colonel Wilkin. "I would state that at the outset one great difficulty existed in the fact that the command was composed of troops of different commands, unacquainted with and distrustful of each other and new to the general commanding " * * * "The enemy met us where common sense would naturally lead them to do so, a few miles from the point in advance, where supplies could be obtained, and yet as far as possible from our base and where the greatest difficulties presented themselves in the way of retreat. Through the medium of the citizens along the route they were of course advised of our force and movements, while we could gain no reliable information in regard to theirs. We were obliged to move on one road, the column extending along the road at least five miles, although well closed up. Attacking our front, they being already formed in line on their own ground, it necessarily took time to bring up our whole force and they had to be moved up rapidly The weather being very warm, many men were obliged to fall out and all came into action more or less fatigued and distressed If they had marched in the cadence and with the proper length of step required by the tactics," * * * "which troops seldom do, they would have been in better condition "

Colonel Waring "The rude character of the country through which we were moving rendered all tactical precautions (except a simple advance guard) impossible; while it was so utterly barren that an immediate .advance or retreat was necessary to procure forage for teams and cavalry horses."

Several officers report that the men of their commands, when hurried into the fight, *were too exhausted to load their pieces.*

General A. J. Smith with two divisions of the 16th Army Corps had touched there in transports and received orders to move against Forrest, destroy as much as possible of the Mobile and Ohio Railroad, and, in short, to retrieve the disaster. His own troops were well seasoned and two brigades of cavalry, in all about 3000, under Grierson, were assigned him. The command numbered about 14,000 men with 50 guns The train was too small to supply the command in a country destitute of everything and it suffered from lack of rations and accommodations for the wounded.

Opposed to it were from 9,000 to 12,000 men under Forrest, nearly all mounted, but fighting habitually on foot. This force was practically without impedimenta, was widely dispersed for subsistence but gathered in Smith's front and on his flanks from all directions as he advanced, being thoroughly familiar with every feature of a most difficult country.

July 5th Smith moved with the infantry, artillery and train from Lagrange, Tennessee, by country roads, towards Spring Hill, Grierson, with all of the cavalry and one battery, from Grand Junction southeast on the Ripley road. Grierson had orders to communicate frequently with the main column, which he did without difficulty.

July 6th. Smith reached the Salem-Ruckersville road, which he could do by several roads from Spring Hill in a formation to resist attack from the front or from the right The cavalry column reached the cross-roads near McLean's Store. Forrest at and beyond Ripley His object was to protect the Mobile and Ohio Railroad by arriving first at any point for which Smith might push and in the mean time to take every opportunity to strike the invading columns if they were unduly lengthened or not within supporting distance of each other.

July 7th. The cavalry to Ripley, dispersing a brigade of the enemy The main column following on the same road, slowly, taking up successive strong positions in line of battle, to the junction of the Ruckersville road, three miles north of Ripley. Forrest on the roads covering the stations at Boonville and Gun Town, and able to reach Rienzi first

July 8th. The main column with one regiment of cavalry towards New-Albany, taking up a strong position on the Tallahatchee,—a force towards Buncomb. The cavalry via Molino to Ellistown and Buncomb. Forrest probably at Old Town. Poplar Spring and Pontotoc.

July 9th-10th Main column advanced slowly to strong position near Cherry Creek The cavalry on the Ellistown-Pontotoc and intermediate roads The enemy apparently concentrating at Pontotoc

July 11th The enemy held Pontotoc with two brigades. Smith attacked them in front and Grierson on their right flank, driving them so precipitately from the position that their dead and wounded were left on the field.

July 12th Smith, willing to be attacked, remained at Pontotoc, the train parked in rear, sending strong reconnoitering parties south and southeast on the roads. The bulk of the cavalry, towards Harrisburg on the road to Tupelo Forrest (as ascertained by one of the reconnoitering parties) in force and strongly intrenched across the Okolona road covering that station and Coonowah: two regiments at Harrisburg. Towards evening of the 12th Smith advanced his pickets, a strong skirmish line and a show of force to within sight of the enemy's lines, built numerous camp fires and appeared even to his own troops, to be making preparations to attack, the next day

July 13th. Soon after midnight the few troops in Forrest's front were withdrawn with every precaution of secrecy towards Pontotoc The cavalry on Tupelo, followed by the main column and train, the latter near the middle of the column and covered on the right flank by a brigade of infantry The march of 18 miles was a forced one and made without any but the most necessary halts The nature of the country to the south rendered flank attacks difficult and in any event they could not be dangerous, while the rapidity of the march enabled a small rear guard of cavalry to repel three attempts to attack from that direction. Early in the afternoon General Grierson occupied Tupelo and the train was at once passed forward and parked two miles west of that place The infantry and batteries followed and by dark had taken up and intrenched a strong position and had begun destroying the railroad

July 14th. Forrest attacked the Federal position with great vigor, twice during the day and once at night, and so gallantly that some of his men penetrated the lines and were captured in rear. The attacks were easily repulsed with excessive loss.*

Smith having destroyed 10 miles of railroad and having only one day's rations on hand, took up his return march to Memphis, reaching Lagrange unmolested on the 21st His total loss was 674, officers and men.

*The Confederate General Buford reports 127 officers killed or wounded and three cap-

Lines of operations. Lines of communications.—Napoleon often used these terms interchangably, sometimes in the same sentence. Since his time the whole subject of lines has been much involved by writers on strategy because it offers a fertile field for analysis and for ingenious combinations, some of which may be demonstrated geometrically on paper. All of these discussions are exceedingly interesting and are thought by many to be instructive. They are open to the objection that they predispose the student to apply exact methods to a science which is extremely impatient of them, but with the warning that they have no direct practical value whatever, they may be studied with undoubted profit. In this study the following summary may serve as a guide.

The line of operations of an army is the system of communications conducting from its base to its objective. It is the general direction followed by its columns, and will have therefore as many good roads and railroads (and, perhaps, waterways) as possible. These roads will also be lines of retreat, and over them will be sent supplies of all kinds; they are therefore lines of communication, also.

As an army advances it may be safer or more convenient to obtain supplies from another quarter and by other roads, either because the line of advance has been excessively lengthened or because the direction of the movable objective has changed. For this reason it has been held that an army may have a line of operations and a line of communications or supply which are separate and distinct. For this reason several writers of note who believe in exact definition, speak of lines of communication only as the lateral or transversal directions which establish communication between lines of march. Having thus disposed of them they are enabled to distinguish between lines of operation and "lines of supply," and to hold that the latter may coincide with the former, may be partially or wholly independent, or may disappear altogether, as in cases where an army subsists on the country entirely or in connection with what supplies can be carried with it.

In practice, however, when an army changes the roads by which it is supplied it changes the direction from which they are received by a wide angle, for, otherwise, there could be no object in the change. It will be obliged to cover and guard these new roads and will use them to all intents and purposes, as part of a line of operations which has simply changed direction.

For these reasons the student may safely assume that terms "*lines of communication,*" "*lines of operations,*" "*lines of supply,*" are *interchangeable, but note in his study of campaigns the few exceptions which may be met:* also take the precaution to ascertain in what sense they are used by his author or whether he confounds them and uses them indiscriminately

It has always been insisted that the most advantageous direction of the lines of operations is that which permits an army to threaten the communications of the enemy without compromising its own Much of this advantage seems to consist in the fact that under the circumstances the enemy is probably unprepared and will, in addition, commit a series of blunders as did the Austrians against Napoleon In 1870 the French were prevented from retreating, before the first battle, towards Paris to Chalons, and concentrating there, by fear of public opinion at the Capital

Napoleon said of lines of operations· "An army marching to the conquest of a country has its two wings protected by neutral territory or large natural obstacles, such as great rivers and large mountain chains; or it has only one of them so protected, or neither of them. In the first case, it has only to watch what takes place in its front; in the second it should support itself upon the protected wing; and in the third it should hold its different corps supported upon the center, and never separate them, for if it is difficult to succeed with two unsupported flanks, this difficulty doubles when there are four flanks; trebles if there are six, and quadruples if there are eight that is to say, if the army is divided into two, three, or four different parts An army's line of operations, in the first instance, may support itself upon the left or the right, indifferently; in the second, it should rest upon the protected wing; in the third, it should be perpendicular to the marching front at the middle point. In every case, it is necessary to have strong places or fortified positions upon the line of operations, at intervals of five or six marches, where supplies of all kinds may be brought together and convoys organized. These places become centers of movement, new startling points whereby the line of operations may be shortened "

In addition to the principles already mentioned Derrécagaix enunciates the following·

"Simple and interior lines of operations are always to be preferred," and he adds·

"The preceeding theories, all of which are the result of experience, should not, however. lead us to forget that the events of war, the nature of the countries traversed, the national spirit of the peoples, and finally the capacity and energy of the leaders, which so powerfully influence the results of a campaign, will never be submitted to fixed maxims nor to preconceived rules."

"War will always be a passionate and bloody drama, not a mathematical operation "

Supply of armies in the field.—This is intimately connected with the subject of wagon transportation, because in nearly all cases wagons must be used in whole or in part The problem ceases to be difficult in proportion as railroads and water transport can be used, and during the War of Secession it was often immeasurably lightened in this way Where an advancing army can be followed up by a line of railroad the task presents, theoretically, no difficulties whatever. practically, however, it is usually hampered by the necessity for guarding the line of road against hostile raids throughout the greater part of its length. From May 1st to November 12th, 1864, General Serman's army of 105,000 soldiers, 30,000 employes, and 35,000 horses, was supplied by a single line of railroad 473 miles long. Trains ran about ten miles per hour, ten cars each, of which four groups of four trains each, were despatched daily—160 cars of ten tons. General Sherman himself says. "To have delivered regularly that amount of food and forage by ordinary wagons would have required 36,800 six mule wagons, allowing each wagon to have hauled two tons twenty miles each day—a simple impossibility." * * * "Therefore I reiterate that the Atlanta Campaign was an impossibility without these railroads."

"If any attempt be made to establish a rule by which to determine the force required to guard an extended line of railroad communications in a hostile country, the exceptions will be more numerous than the cases to which the rule will apply. If an army advances leaving any considerable force of the enemy in the rear, it will be simply impossible to secure efficient protection to communications: for however numerous may be the force detailed for protection, it will always be possible for an enemy to concentrate a superior force upon a given point and effect a temporary break. The reliance in such cases must be in the rapidity of reconstruction. In this we were far in advance of the enemy ' "General Sherman had such confidence in its efficiency that he would advance with a feeling of assurance that if his communications were broken they would be established before any serious suffering could result therefrom. Our rule was, where we could not get the material that we wanted, to take such as we could get. Trees, buildings and fences usually furnished sufficient material. We could not prevent communications from being broken, but they were restored with great celerity."*

The number of men per mile for guarding a line of communication is exceedingly variable—depending on the topography of the country and the disposition of the inhabitants. According to the Germans about 1,000 men are required for each stretch of a day's march—say 15 miles At this rate an army 60 miles from its base would require 4,000 Assume one line for each corps of 40,000 and the proportion of the army necessary to guard its own communications is one-tenth, (doubling the length one-fifth, trippling one-third, &c.) But General Sheridan, who speaks from personel observation, considered the German lines very ineffectively protected and he claimed that with comparatively small forces of American cavalry he could have kept them broken, 1 e., he could have rendered the German advance impossible or hampered it so seriously as to necessitate entire change of plans He criticised the French mounted troops severely for not doing this

In the Atlanta Campaign Sherman's main base was Louisville, Kentucky. Supplies for the Depot (Magazine) at Nashville were mainly received 183 miles by rail from there—aided by river communication where the heighth of the water permitted. South of Nashville communication was by railroad alone. Taking his line at 480 miles and the number of troops engaged in guarding it we have roughly about 1,500 per fifteen miles For reasons already indicated these were very unevenly distributed—north of Chattanooga about 550—south about 3.500 per fifteen miles. Portions of the road easy to destroy and hard to reconstruct were guarded by blockhouses with garrisons of from twenty men to a company—capable of protracted defence· most important railway stations were intrenched camps—the whole patrolled constantly by a tireless cavalry. Nashville, Chattanooga and Allatoona were fortified garrisons provisioned as contingent bases "To supply 100 000 men in the field, with a single track, the proportion of rolling stock should be 0.25 engines and six freight cars per mile of road."

· According to General Sherman no army depending entirely on wagons can operate more than 100 miles from its base because the teams going and coming consume the contents of the wagons

This statement has been put in analytical form as follows·

"One six mule wagon will carry supplies for 500 men for one day "

---
* Haupt.

"Since it must return to refill, if the troops are one day's march from their base it will supply only 250 men: it follows that if the troops are two days march from their base four wagons are required for 500 men—or 800 wagons for 100,000 men. But with 100,000 men there would be about 16,000 cavalry and artillery horses, and these require 800 additional wagons, with about 5000 animals the wagons consume practically one day at the base in loading, and additional animals require additional wagons for forage, &c. Figuring on this basis we can find that an army of 100,000 men a little over 100 miles from its base would require about 10,000 wagons drawn by about 65,000 animals. This would be a train over 100 miles long, under favorable conditions "*

As the wagons, therefore, excepting within very narrow limits, cannot return to the base of supplies to refill, it is necessary to keep these limits narrow, as the army advances by moving up the base—or in other words by establishing secondary bases, or transition stations, utilizing railroad and water supply, as far in the direction of the advance as possible, and establishing depots and magazines strongly placed and guarded, at such points as may be available. These magazines and depots are:

1. Principal. at the base of operations
2. Secondary: on the line of operations.
3. Provisional: in the immediate neighborhood of the troops, with supplies for a few days only.

May 4th, 1864. The Army of the Potomac, 150,000 strong, left Brandy Station, (Rappahannock River near Culpepper.) Base had been at Alexandria—50 miles by rail. It was to cut loose from base, carrying rations for about sixteen days, or until new base could be established."

"Soldiers carried three days rations in knapsacks. in haversacks three days hard bread, coffee, sugar and salt. Supply trains carried ten days rations of these articles and one day's ration of salt pork. Thirteen days meat ration was driven on the hoof."

"If this train loaded with this modified ration and with ammunition and stores were placed in one line it would have extended from Washington to Richmond—about 130 miles. Subsistence was packed in each wagon. forty boxes hard bread: or pork six barrels, coffee four barrels: or sugar ten barrels. salt, one sack per wagon—displacing a barrel of sugar or coffee."

* Sharpe

"May 8th. (After the Wilderness), five days rations issued and empty wagons sent to Fredericksburg to be reloaded."

"May 11th Five days rations issued (1 days salt meat.) Empty wagons sent to Belle-Plain, where a depot for subsistence had been established, to be reloaded to maximum capacity, including three days salt meat."

"May 13th. Rations issued to include 19th Wagons sent to Belle-Plain"

"May 20th. Troops moved from Spottsylvania Court House and crossed N. Anna on 21st. Trains withdrawn from Fredericksburg, Depot at Belle-Plain broken up· temporary depot at Port Royal, thirty miles from army. supply trains packed to Milford, (fourteen miles) Troops with four days rations· supply train with eight."

"May 31st. Depot removed from Port Royal and established at White House—where empty trains were sent for supplies."

"June 4th. Three days rations issued—giving five days from June 5th On both days, June 7th and 9th, two days rations issued"

"June 10th An order required the men to have always four days rations, and that six days be kept in division supply train: surplus wagons to carry fresh vegetables, antiscorbutics, &c."

"During this march the principal base may be considered to have been the Potomac River, Alexandria, &c., the secondary bases at Fredericksburg, Belle-Plain, Port Royal, &c., the provisional basis being the main supply train, from which the division trains replenished."

"When the army reached the James River and crossed, City Point became the base of supplies, and the task of supplying the army during the march ceased—the depot being very near and accessible."*

Service may be by continuous convoy, alternate relays (wagons unpacked) or successive relays. Where the Germans drove the enemy in front of them leaving a thickly settled country with good roads in their rear, these methods could be systematically applied. They had per corps—80 wagons supplying current rations, 80 in reserve, 400 between these two and the temporary magazines—600 to keep the temporary magazines supplied. Total, 1,160

Grant had about thirty-five wagons per 1,000 men after crossing the Rapidan, but he carried ten days full rations in the supply train, three days beef on the hoof, three days full rations in

---
* Sharpe

the haversacks and three days hard bread in the knapsacks. This would give him a modified supply for about fifteen days. If the men husband their hard bread (which they should be made to do) they often get along with very little else,—being satisfied with the fresh meat found in the country and with coffee, sugar and salt. After Antietam McClellan had about thirty-two wagons per 1,000 men, but they carried seven days full rations, and eight days (modified ration.)

Transportation can be reduced and was frequently reduced during the War of Secession as follows:

1st. By carrying no tents excepting very few for office purposes.

2nd By driving cattle on the hoof, including many gathered en route, for the meat ration.

3rd. By reducing the rest of the ration, excepting hard bread to about one-half, for short periods

4th. By using up the supplies in a certain number of wagons and sending these back as they became empty as long as possible.

5th. By carrying no special supplies for officers and no officer's baggage.

On Roussean's raid no vehicle whatever was taken, excepting some ambulances. Ammunition, mess-pans and camp kettles were packed on mules. The men carried in their haversacks fifteen days rations of coffee, salt and sugar, five of hard bread and one of bacon,—no blankets and no extra clothing. (July, 1864.)

The proportion of men to animals, in an army, including the cavalry horses and spare horses, seems to be about three and one-half to one

CPSIA information can be obtained at www.ICGtesting.com
Printed in the USA
BVOW06*1854171215

430560BV00002B/4/P